7 AFRICAN AMERICAN SCIENTISTS

Achievers: African Americans In Science and Technology

7 AFRICAN
AMERICAN
SCIENTISTS

Robert C. Hayden

Twenty-First Century Books

Brookfield, Connecticut

Twenty-First Century Books
A Division of The Millbrook Press, Inc.
2 Old New Milford Road
Brookfield, Connecticut 06804

Cover photo by Telegraph Colour Library/FPG International
Portrait illustrations by Richard Loehle
Photos pp. 24 & 27 courtesy of the American Antiquarian Society

Library of Congress Cataloging-in-Publication Data

Hayden, Robert C.
7 African-American Scientists
Illustrated by Richard Loehle

Includes index.

Summary: Examines the lives and achievements of seven black
Americans who left their mark through scientific work.

1. Afro-American scientists—Biography—Juvenile literature.
[1. Scientists. 2. Afro-Americans—Biography.] I. Loehle, Richard,
ill. II. Title. III. Title: Seven African-American scientists. IV. Title:
African-American scientists. V. Series: Hayden, Robert C.,
Achievers: African Americans in Science and Technology.

Q141.H37 1992 509.2′273—dc20 [B] 91-44194 CIP AC
ISBN 0-8050-2134-5

Printed in the United States of America

10 9 8 7

CON

FOREWORD

A book on the contributions of African Americans to American science should really begin in ancient Africa. Contrary to popular belief, the African ancestors of today's African Americans had great control over the natural and physical world. That is, they could explain and predict the way things worked in their world. They knew how to use animal and plant materials for proper nourishment. They knew how to cure diseases and illnesses. They explored the uses of natural substances found in the earth. They knew how to use the natural energy sources of water, air, and fire.

Who were the ancient ancestors of today's African-American scientists?

They were chemists, explorers, and engineers. They were mathematicians and agricultural experts. They were botanists and animal scientists.

- Between 1,500 and 2,000 years ago, Africans in Tanzania were producing carbon steel.

- The early Dogon people of West Africa left paintings that show the rings of Saturn and the moons of Jupiter.

- Building the pyramids of Egypt and the massive stone structures in Zimbabwe required extensive knowledge of mathematics.

- Archaeological evidence reveals that the scientific cultivation of crops occurred in Africa at least 7,000 years before it did on any other continent.

- Africans had their own medicines. The Bantu-speaking people in central Africa used the bark of the salix tree to treat muscle and joint pains. The tree contains salicylic acid, a main ingredient in the modern aspirin tablet.

Americans of African descent have a heritage of such scientific interests and progress. Just as African-American men and women have made important contributions to sports, literature, politics, the military, education, business, and the worlds of music and entertainment, so they also have a long record of achievement in science. These accomplishments, however, are not generally known by either white or black Americans.

In 1939, a committee was formed in New York City to select the most outstanding African Americans in the history of the United States. Forty-two people were chosen, and their names were placed on a panel in the Hall of Fame at the New York World's Fair in 1940.

Included on that list are the names of three men who distinguished themselves in the field of natural science— Benjamin Banneker (1731-1806), George Washington Carver (1864-1943), and Ernest E. Just (1883-1941). To this list of three, I have added the names of four more African Americans who have also left their mark through scientific work—Charles H. Turner (1867-1923), Matthew Henson (1865-1955), Percy Julian (1899-1975), and Shirley Jackson (1946-).

Despite the fact that only a small percentage of the scientists in the history of the United States have been African Americans, these men and women worked in and contributed to a broad range of scientific studies, from astronomy to entomology, from agriculture to physics.

You will learn how Dr. Ernest E. Just revolutionized our understanding of the nature of living material, how Dr. Charles Henry Turner studied the behavior of insects, how Matthew Henson co-discovered the North Pole, and how George Washington Carver developed new commercial products from the peanut. You will learn that Benjamin Banneker was studying astronomy in the 1700s, that Dr. Percy Julian created synthetic medicines in the 1940s and

1950s, and that today Dr. Shirley Jackson, a theoretical physicist, studies and explains the behavior of materials that are used to improve our communications systems.

This book is about seven African-American pioneers in science. It is about their lives and the challenges they faced. It is about their work and the contributions they have made to scientific research.

As you read these biographies, you will see that each of these people possessed two qualities central to scientific inquiry—curiosity and determination.

One may ask why these seven scientists and their work were chosen as the subject for a book. The answer lies in the fact that so little has been written in the past about African Americans in science. The contributions to knowledge made by these researchers are significant and even revolutionary. Yet information about them and their work is missing from most science books. Details about them and their scientific contributions are scattered and difficult to obtain. Only one of them, Matthew Henson, left an autobiography to help the present-day writer of the history of science.

Being a scientist is not easy. Scientists fail as well as succeed as they question old beliefs and try to discover new truths. They often face the problem of getting people to give attention to their work and to accept new information and ideas.

Scientists who are black face these same problems along with the added problems that are caused by racial prejudice and discrimination.

What has it meant to be both a scientist and an African American?

What have been some of the accomplishments of African Americans in the sciences?

This book aims to answer these questions.

> Robert C. Hayden
> Boston, Massachusetts
> 1992

BENJAMIN BANNEKER

1

His neighbors called him a "lazy old man." When they peeped into his cabin during the day, they saw him sound asleep. They talked about his peculiar living habits and how he had changed. In his younger days, he put in a full day's work every day on his farm near the city of Baltimore, Maryland. But he no longer tended cows or tilled the soil the way he used to. Good farmers, his neighbors said, should be up and working early and in bed soon after dark.

Little did his neighbors know that at night, while they slept, Benjamin Banneker was awake and outdoors. Not laziness, but astronomy accounted for his daytime sleep.

Each night, as darkness approached, Banneker would leave his cabin. Wrapped in a cloak, he would lie flat on his back most of the night, gazing at heavenly bodies with his telescope. He was studying the motions of the moon, sun, stars, and planets. At sunrise, he would return to his cabin and go to bed. Throughout the morning hours, while everyone else was hard at work, Benjamin Banneker was sound asleep. Occasionally during the afternoon, he would hoe his small garden and trim his fruit trees.

During the day, when he wasn't sleeping, Benjamin Banneker was shut up in his cabin. Alone, he was studying astronomy books and making calculations. In fact, he was so immersed in his studies that neighborhood boys would trespass on his land and strip his trees of their fruit without his even noticing.

Even the cold winter nights did not stop Banneker from making his astronomical observations. From a window he made in the roof of his cabin, he could still observe the night sky during the winter. He did not worry about the neighbors gossiping about his daily routine. He was too busy with his nightly gazing and daily calculations.

During the 1700s, few white men seriously studied science books. Very few considered science, much less astronomy, as an occupation. For an African American to be studying the sun, moon, stars, and planets—that was very unusual!

In 1791, James McHenry, a prominent politician in Maryland, sent the following letter to Goddard and Angell, owners of a publishing company in Baltimore:

Baltimore, August 20, 1791

Messrs. Goddard and Angell,

BENJAMIN BANNEKER, a free Negro, has calculated an Almanac, for the coming year, 1792. He desires to put it to good use and has requested me to aid his application to have it published. I have satisfied myself with respect to his title to this kind of authorship. If you can agree with him on a price for his work, I can assure you that it will do you credit. At the same time, you will be encouraging Banneker's talents that have thus far surmounted the most discouraging circumstances and prejudice.

This man is about fifty-nine years of age. He was born in Baltimore County. His father was an African, and his mother the offspring of African parents. His father and mother, having obtained their freedom, were able to send him to an obscure school, where he learned, as a boy, reading, writing, and arithmetic. At their death, his parents left him a few acres of farm land. From his farming he has supported himself ever since by means of constant labor and producing fine crops.

What he learned at school, he did not forget. During hours of leisure which occurred during his most toilsome farm life, he worked at mathematical problems, applying the principles of the few rules of arithmetic he had been taught at school. This kind of mental exercise formed his chief amusement. His facility with arithmetical calculations made him often serviceable to his neighbors. He attracted the attention of the Ellicott family, known for their remarkable ingenuity and knowledge in mechanics. It is about three years since George Ellicott lent Banneker some of his books and tables on astronomy and some astronomical instruments. From thenceforth, he employed his leisure in astronomical researches.

He now took up the idea of the calculations for an Almanac, and actually completed an entire set for the last year, upon his original stock of arithmetic. Encouraged by his first attempt, he entered upon his calculation for 1792. His latest Almanac, as well as the former, he began and finished without the least information, or assistance, from any person, or other books than those from Mr. Ellicott. So whatever merit is attached to his present performance, is exclusively and peculiarly his own. . . .

I consider this Negro as a fresh proof that the powers of the mind are disconnected with color of the skin. . . . In every civilized country we shall find thousands of whites, liberally educated, and who have enjoyed greater opportunities of instruction than this Negro. Yet many [whites] are inferior to him in those intellectual acquirements and capacities that form the most characteristic feature in the human race.

The system that would assign to these degraded blacks an origin different from whites must be relinquished as similar circumstances multiply. Banneker is a striking contradiction to the doctrine that "the Negroes are naturally inferior to whites, and unsusceptible to accomplishments in arts and sciences." If nothing is to impede the progress of humanity, then bettering the condition of slavery will necessarily lead to its extinction. Let, however, the issue be what it may, I cannot but wish, on this occasion, to see the public patronage keep pace with my black friend's merit.

I am, Gentlemen, your most obedient servant,

James McHenry

So it was that Benjamin Banneker, at 60 years of age, had his first *Almanac* published for the year 1792. And each year afterward until 1802, Banneker's *Almanac* was published. For an African American in the 1790s, this was a remarkable scientific achievement. Banneker's *Almanac* was widely read in Pennsylvania, Delaware, Maryland, Virginia, and in other states. In many homes, it was found next to the family Bible.

Benjamin Banneker's *Almanac* contained calculations that showed a high scientific and mathematical ability. In addition to being a guidebook to the heavenly events of the time, almanacs were a source of weather and tidal information. Weather forecasts were important to farmers and to travelers during the time, just as they are today. Essays on nature in Banneker's *Almanac* were based on his own sharp-eyed observations.

Hands in the Dirt, Head in the Clouds

Few of the facts and events of Benjamin Banneker's early life are known. What is known was recorded in his family's Bible.

Benjamin Banneker was born free of slavery in the thinly populated countryside of Maryland, about 10 miles from Baltimore. He was raised and lived all of his life on his family's farm that bordered the Patapsco River. His parents, who were free black people (his father had been a slave who purchased his freedom), bought the 102 acres of farmland in 1737 with 17,000 pounds of tobacco. On a hill overlooking the river, Benjamin's father built the family home. Benjamin was six years old at the time.

The Banneker farm was known to be one of the best in the community, producing vegetables, fruit, poultry, and honey from beehives. Farming was the sole means by which Benjamin Banneker's father was able to support his family of six. Throughout his boyhood, young Benjamin worked side by side with his parents, helping in the daily chores of farm life. He could attend school only during the winter, when there was little farm work to be done.

In a one-room school, Benjamin Banneker learned how to read, write, and do simple mathematics. He was very good at solving mathematical problems. Benjamin's eagerness for books and learning was seen early in his life. Young Banneker seldom played with his schoolmates, preferring instead to read whatever books he could get hold of. Few books were available when Banneker was a boy. It was difficult for anyone—white or black—to get a good education at that time.

Despite his studious habits, young Benjamin became an industrious and excellent farmer. But while he worked hard with his hands in the soil, his brain was hard at work making up and solving problems in mathematics. The farming community in which he lived provided little opportunity for scholars, white or black. But it seems that Banneker was able to overcome these obstacles—the lack of books at home and the little schooling he received—by learning things firsthand.

He had an intense curiosity and was a close observer of everything in nature—the sky, earth, clouds, rain, and the seasons. And Banneker had a reputation in the local community for being extremely intelligent, with a quick and sharp mind for working with numbers.

News of Benjamin Banneker's mathematical ability soon spread throughout the county and into surrounding states. Farmers came to him with brain-testing puzzles and practical problems to solve.

A Clock Made of Hardwood

By the age of 22, Benjamin Banneker had finished constructing a clock. It was the first of its kind in the Maryland region. Its construction gave him a chance to apply some of his mathematical ability and demonstrated his genius for mechanics.

It is reported that Banneker took apart and studied the pieces of a pocket watch made in England and lent to him by a traveling merchant. He used the watch as a model for his clock. The parts of this clock, which struck at the hours of 6 and 12, were made of hardwood that was cut and shaped with a knife. He had no delicate tools to help him fashion such an intricate mechanism.

The building of the clock turned out to be of great importance in the life of Benjamin Banneker. By 1772, the clock had been keeping time for about 20 years. Its fame attracted the attention of neighbors throughout Baltimore County. People in Maryland, Delaware, Pennsylvania, and Virginia heard about the clock built by a "colored" man. They traveled great distances to see it.

Banneker enjoyed the company of these visitors since he was unmarried and lived alone on the farm that he had inherited from his parents. Visitors described Banneker as a "brave-looking pleasant man . . . noble in appearance. . . . A perfect gentleman . . . kind, generous, hospitable, humane, dignified, and pleasing to talk with."

Among those who came to see Banneker's famous clock were members of the distinguished Ellicott family—George, Andrew, John, and Benjamin. The Ellicotts were a well-educated Quaker family with engineering, scientific, and business talent. They had moved from Pennsylvania and settled near Banneker's farm in 1772 to build and operate flour mills along the Patapsco River. While living in Pennsylvania, they heard about their neighbor's clock.

Benjamin Banneker spent many hours watching the construction of the Ellicotts' flour mills and the operation of the mill machinery. The Ellicotts' flour business grew rapidly. A store and post office were soon opened at the mill site. Supplies sold at the store and food for the mill workers came from Banneker's farm. Today, Ellicott City stands at the site of the Ellicott flour enterprise near the Patapsco River in Maryland.

A New World

Having the Ellicotts as neighbors was a turning point in Benjamin Banneker's life. The store and post office were popular meeting places for people to discuss the news of the day. George Ellicott, a mathematician and astronomer, was impressed by the curiosity and scientific interests of his African-American neighbor and respected Banneker's mechanical genius and aptitude for science and mathematics. The common interests of Benjamin Banneker and George Ellicott led them into a strong friendship.

George Ellicott encouraged the interests and talents of his new friend by lending him a number of astronomy books and instruments. Among the books were Mayer's *Tables of the Sun and Moon*, Leadbetter's *Lunar Tables*, and Ferguson's *Astronomy*. These books, important and scholarly works of the time, were the first of their kind that Benjamin Banneker had ever seen. They opened up a new world to him.

George Ellicott had intended to instruct Banneker in how to use the rather difficult books, but he never got around to it. That didn't slow Banneker down for long, however. Ellicott was later surprised to find that Banneker had discovered how to use the books even without his assistance. Within a few years, Banneker could predict when eclipses of the sun and moon would occur.

The study of astronomy captured Banneker's interest and came to dominate his life completely. In studying the books given to him by his friend, Banneker claimed to have found errors of calculation. He mentioned some of these errors in notes to George Ellicott. One of his notes read as follows:

> It appears to me that the wisest men may at times be in error; for instance, Dr. Ferguson informs us that, when the sun is within 12° of either node at the time of full moon, the moon will be eclipsed; but I find that, according to his method of projecting a lunar eclipse, there will be none by the above elements, and yet the sun is within 11° 468' 11" of the moon's ascending node. But the moon, being in her apogee, prevents the appearance of this eclipse.

As the years moved on, Benjamin Banneker advanced in his astronomical studies. George Ellicott urged him to undertake the calculations of an almanac. To do so, Banneker would have to give up farming and spend all of his time studying astronomy and mathematics. And this he did, at the age of 52, by selling his farm to the Ellicotts. They paid him enough money each year thereafter to live on and allowed him to continue living in the cabin that he had occupied all of his life.

Free of laborious farming chores, Benjamin Banneker could now study the heavens at night and sleep and do his calculations during the day. For the next 20 years, he devoted all of his time to the science of astronomy.

Before 1790, Benjamin Banneker had never traveled very far from his farm, much less outside of his home state of Maryland. His fame was local, but national recognition was in his future.

A Capital City

In 1790, the United States established the nation's capital city on the Potomac River. Portions of land from the states of Maryland and Virginia were relinquished by those states to make up the new Federal Territory (now Washington, D.C.). President George Washington selected a team of civil engineers and surveyors to lay out the streets of the new capital and to plan the location of the new government buildings.

One of the Ellicott brothers, Major Andrew Ellicott, was appointed to the survey commission. Andrew Ellicott, knowing Banneker's talents, suggested to Thomas Jefferson, then secretary of state, that Benjamin Banneker be named to assist him in laying out the Federal Territory.

Thus, President Washington, at Thomas Jefferson's suggestion, appointed Benjamin Banneker to the federal commission that would plan and lay out the capital of the United States. On March 12, 1791, the *Georgetown Weekly Ledger* noted the arrival of Ellicott and Pierre L'Enfant (a famous French engineer who headed the commission), accompanied by "Benjamin Banneker, an Ethiopian whose abilities as surveyor and astronomer already prove that [the conclusion] that that race of men were void of mental endowment was without foundation."

Benjamin Banneker helped in selecting the sites for the U.S. Capitol building, the U.S. Treasury building, the White House, and other federal buildings. When L'Enfant quit his job as head of the commission over a dispute with federal officials, he left and took the printed plans for the city with him. President Washington was afraid that the commission's work on the new federal city would come to a standstill. But Benjamin Banneker had memorized the plans that he, Ellicott, and L'Enfant had worked out. So the job was able to be finished without L'Enfant.

At that time, most African Americans in this country were held as slaves. Benjamin Banneker showed that free African Americans with much less formal education than many whites could make significant contributions to the development, life, and culture of the new nation.

When he was not surveying and laying out the streets of the District of Columbia, Banneker was hard at work with his astronomical investigations. On his return from the federal city, Banneker completed his first *Almanac.*

JANUARY, MDCCXCV.

ON HAPPINESS.

O Happineſs ! where's thy reſort?
 Amidſt the ſplendors of a court?
Or doſt thou more delight to dwell,
With humble merit in his cell,
In ſearch of truth? Or doſt thou rove
Thro' Plato's academic grove ?

D.M.	D.W.	Remarkable Days, Aſpects, Judgment of weather, &c.	Sun riſes. H.M.	Sun ſets. H.M.	M's place.	A Scrap.
1	5	Circumciſion.	7 20	4 40	♉ 23	The wiſeſt of
2	6	☌ ☉ ♀ orient.	7 20	4 40	♊ 7	thoſe who live is he who be-
3	7	wind with	7 20	4 40	♊ 1	lieves himſelf
4	D	flying clouds.	7 19	4 41	♋ 5	the neareſt to
5	2	☌ ☉ ♃ orient.	7 19	4 41	19	death and re-
6	3	Epiphany.	7 18	4 42	♌ 3	gulates all his
7	4	rain	7 18	4 42	16	actions by that
8	5	Pleiades ſouth 8 15.	7 17	4 43	29	thought.
9	6	or ſnow,	7 17	4 43	♍ 11	The moſt
10	7	Days increaſe 12m.	7 16	4 44	24	ſenſible on the
11	D	1ſt. Sun. paſt Epip.	7 15	4 45	♎ 6	contrary, a-
12	2	☌ ☉ ♄	7 15	4 45	18	mong thoſe
13	3	cold	7 14	4 46	29	who make ſci-
14	4	Days 9h. 34m.	7 13	4 47	♏ 11	entific ſearch-
15	5	weather,	7 13	4 47	23	es, is he who
16	6	Sirius South 10 41.	7 12	4 48	♐ 5	believes him-
17	7	ſnow.	7 11	4 49	18	ſelf the far-
18	D	2d. Sun. paſt Epip.	7 10	4 50	♑ 1	theſt from the
19	2	☌ ♃ ☿, ☌ ☽ ☉ ♃	7 10	4 50	14	goal, and who
20	3	☉ en ♒ ☉ ecl. inv.	7 9	4 51	27	whatever ad-
21	4	windy	7 8	4 52	♒ 11	vances he has
22	5	♀ Stationary.	7 7	4 53	24	made in his
23	6	♄ Stationary.	7 6	4 54	♓ 8	road, ſtudies
24	7	cloudy	7 5	4 55	22	as if he yet
25	D	3d. Sun. paſt Epip.	7 4	4 56	♈ 7	knew nothing
26	2	and	7 3	4 57	21	and marches
27	3	Pleiades ſets 2 18.	7 2	4 58	♉ 5	as if he were
28	4	cold,	7 1	4 59	20	only yet be-
29	5	Days increaſe 44m.	7 0	5 0	♊	ginning to
30	6	Snow or rain.	6 59	5 1	18	make his firſt
31	7	Sirius South 9 38.	6 58	5 2	♋ 1	advances.

With the help of James McHenry, Banneker arranged for the publication of his work in 1792.

Banneker's *Almanac*

An almanac is a book or table with a calendar of days and months to which astronomical information is added. It shows the times of the rising and setting of the sun and moon, phases of the moon, positions of planets, eclipses, the times of high and low tides, and other useful items of information about the natural environment. With information from an almanac as a guide, a farmer could reset a stopped clock, tell the time of day, and estimate the proper time of season to plant and harvest his crops.

The compiling of almanacs began thousands of years ago when astronomy began to develop as a science. The first printed almanac appeared in 1457. It was a German astronomer who produced the almanac that was used by the explorer Christopher Columbus. The first American almanac was printed in Massachusetts in 1639.

Banneker calculated his almanacs for each year from 1792 to 1802. The almanacs were printed—and they sold well—throughout that period. In each edition, he included tables with the following information:

- the motions of the sun and moon

- the true places and aspects of the planets

- the rising and setting of the sun

- the rising, setting, and southing of the moon

- lunations, conjunctions, and eclipses

- the rising, setting, and southing of the planets

- noted fixed stars

A copy of a page from Benjamin Banneker's *Almanac* for 1795 can be found on page 24. His almanacs carried a table of information like this for each month of the year.

Besides astronomical calculations, there were other items of unusual interest in Banneker's almanacs. One of these was a horoscope, as shown on page 27. A horoscope is a diagram that divides the heavens into 12 parts. Each part is governed by one of 12 different constellations, or groups of stars. The ancient Greeks identified animals or objects with each of these constellations, according to the figures they saw as they looked at the different groups of stars. Here are the names of the constellations with their popular names (or "signs") beside them:

ARIES—The Ram
TAURUS—The Bull
GEMINI—The Twins
CANCER—The Crab
LEO—The Lion
VIRGO—The Virgin
LIBRA—The Scales
SCORPIO—The Scorpion
SAGITTARIUS—The Archer
CAPRICORN—The Goat
AQUARIUS—The Waterman
PISCES—The Fishes

The Anatomy of Man's Body, as governed by the Twelve Constellations.

Characters, &c. of the Constellations.

♈ Aries, a Ram, the Head & Face.
♉ Taurus, a Bull, the Neck.
♊ Gemini, the Twins, the Arms.
♋ Cancer, a Crab, the Breast.
♌ Leo, a Lion, the Heart.
♍ Virgo, a Virgin, the Bowels.

♎ Libra, a Balance, the Reins
♏ Scor. a Scorpion, the Secrets
♐ Sag. a Bowman, the Thighs
♑ Capricorn, a Goat, the Knees
♒ Aquarius, a Butler, the Legs
♓ Pisces, the Fish, the Feet.

To know where the Sign is. First find the day of the month, and against it you have the sign or place of the moon in the sixth column. Then finding the sign here, it shews the part of the body it governs.

Count the number of figures or signs drawn around the figure of the human body on page 27. This illustration reflects the thinking that each constellation has an effect on the condition of a different part of the human body. The idea that groups of stars are able to influence parts of the body is a very ancient one. It probably originated thousands of years ago with the first stargazers.

Here is the explanation of the horoscope as written by Banneker. As you read each line, look at the illustration and find the signs that he is referring to:

> Man's head and face Heaven's ram obey
> His neck the neck-strong bull does sway
> The arm-twining twins guide hands and arms
> Breasts, sides, and stomach Cancer charms
> The lion rules his back and heart
> Bowels and belly's Virgo's part
> Veins, haunches, navel, Libra tends
> Bladder and secrets Scorpio befriends
> The half-hors'd bowman rules the thighs
> And to the goat our knees suffice
> Our legs are but the butler's fees
> The fish our footsteps oversees.

Some ancient astronomers thought that they had also discovered a close relationship between the movements of the heavenly bodies and human events. This early kind of thinking was called astrology. Over the centuries, however, with the rise of modern science, astrology has come to be known as a false or sham science (a pseudoscience). It is interesting to note, though, that in recent years, there has been a renewed interest in astrology. Many newspapers now carry a daily horoscope.

Letter to the President

Benjamin Banneker became famous in his time for the astronomical calculations presented in his almanacs. But Banneker was more than a successful, self-taught scientist and mathematician.

Although he was himself a free man, Banneker was aware of and deeply troubled by slavery and the racist treatment received by black people in America. He was concerned about the attitudes of public officials toward the plight of his race in America.

In the late 1700s, racial restrictions were being used to oppress free blacks as well as slaves. During the last years of his life, Benjamin Banneker could not vote. Some whites were beginning to fear free, educated blacks even more than slaves.

Banneker was one of the first African Americans to speak out for the cause of racial equality and the abolition of slavery. When Banneker presented a handwritten copy of his first *Almanac* to Thomas Jefferson, the author of the Declaration of Independence, he used the opportunity to advance the cause of African Americans.

Thomas Jefferson was a slave owner. Along with the copy of his *Almanac*, Banneker sent a letter to Jefferson, dated August 19, 1791, in which he wrote the following plea for racial understanding:

> We are a race of beings who have long labored under the abuse and censure of the world. . . . We have long been considered rather as brutish than human, and scarcely capable of mental endowments.

Sir, I hope . . . that you are a man far less inflexible in sentiments of this nature than many others, that you are measurably friendly and well disposed toward us. . . .

Now, Sir . . . I apprehend that your sentiments are concurrent with mine, which are that our universal Father hath given being to all. . . . But, Sir, how pitiable it is to reflect that, although you were so fully convinced of the benevolence of the Father of mankind . . . that you should at the same time counteract His mercies in detaining by fraud and violence so numerous a part of my brethren under groaning captivity and cruel oppression. . . .

Suffer me, Sir, to recall . . . that when the tyranny of the British crown was exerted to reduce you to servitude, your abhorrence was so excited that you publicly held forth this true and invaluable doctrine: . . . "We hold these truths to be self-evident, that all men are created equal, and that they are endowed by their Creator with certain inalienable rights; that among these are life, liberty, and pursuit of happiness." . . .

The Almanac is a production of my arduous study. I have long had unbounded desires to become acquainted with the secrets of nature, and I have had to gratify my curiosity herein through my own assiduous application to astronomical study. I need not recount to you the many difficulties and disadvantages I have had to encounter. I conclude by subscribing myself, with the most profound respect, your most humble servant,

B. Banneker

This letter made Jefferson uncomfortable, but it also impressed him. Jefferson sent the almanac to Marquis de Condorcet, the secretary of the Academy of Sciences in Paris, to prove that the color of a person's skin has nothing to do with intelligence. "I am happy to inform you that we have now in the United States a Negro . . . who is a very respectable mathematician," he wrote to Condorcet.

To Benjamin Banneker, Jefferson wrote the following letter in reply:

> Sir, I thank you sincerely for your letter, and for the Almanac it contained. Nobody wishes more than I do to see such proofs as you exhibit that nature has given to our black brethren talents equal to those of the other colors of men, and that the appearance of want of them is owing only to the degraded condition of their existence both in Africa and America. I can add, with truth, that no one wishes more ardently to see a good system commenced for raising the condition both of their body and mind to what it ought to be, as fast as . . . current circumstances, which cannot be neglected, will admit. I have taken the liberty of sending your almanac to Monsieur Condorcet, Secretary of the Academy of Sciences at Paris, and to members of the Philanthropic Society, because I considered it a document to which your whole color had a right, for their justification against the doubts which have been entertained of them. I am, with great esteem, sir, your most obedient servant,
>
> Thomas Jefferson

Benjamin Banneker was a self-taught mathematician, astronomer, surveyor, and mechanic. But he was more.

Banneker was also a humanitarian.

He cared intensely about the quality of life for African Americans who were enslaved. And he spoke out boldly in his letters and conversations with the nation's leaders for the humane treatment of his people.

Banneker's Legacy

After 1802, Benjamin Banneker was too old and feeble to continue the calculation of almanacs. He died in 1806, and he was buried near the cabin that had been both his lifetime home and the place where he had carried out all of his scientific work.

The *Federal Gazette* and *Baltimore Daily Advertiser*, each dated October 28, 1806, printed the following notice of Banneker's death:

> On Sunday, the 25th, departed from this life, near his residence in Baltimore County, Mr. Benjamin Banneker, a black man, immediate descendant of an African father. He was known in this neighborhood for his quiet and peaceful demeanor and among scientific men, as an astronomer and mathematician.

Benjamin Banneker demonstrated to a slave-holding nation that blacks are a part of the human family. His own scientific achievements were proof that the idea of the inferiority of black people of African descent should be destroyed. Banneker's life was a search for independence.

In 1797, nine years before Benjamin Banneker died, the following poem appeared in his *Almanac*. It could serve as a fitting tribute to Benjamin Banneker himself:

Epitaph for a Watch-Maker

Here lies, in a horizontal position,
The outside case of
Peter Pendulum, Watch-Maker
Whose abilities in that line were an honour
To his profession.
Integrity was the main spring
And prudence was the regulator
Of all the actions of his life.
Humane, generous and liberal
His hand never stopped
Till he had relieved distress.

So nicely regulated were all his motions
 That he never went wrong
  Except when set a-going
   By people
 Who did not know
  His key!
 Even then he was easily
  Set right again.
He had the art of disposing his time
 So well,
  That his hours glided away,
   In one continual round
   Of pleasures and delights
Till an unlucky minute put a period to
 His existence.
 He departed this life
  Wound up
 In hope of being taken in hand
  By his Maker
And of being thoroughly cleaned, repaired,
   And set a-going
 In the world to come.

CHARLES HENRY TURNER

2

His stomach was pressed against the bare brown earth. He was lying flat on the ground watching some ants. His eyes were only four inches from the dirt. The ants were very busy. One by one, they moved in and out of their tiny hole in the ground. They seemed to know exactly where they were going.

Some ants would take long trips away from the anthill around the hole, but they would always find their way home without getting lost. How mysterious all this was, thought Charles H. Turner, his eyes fixed intently on the ants moving around the hole. The movements of the ants fascinated him, particularly their sense of direction. Their actions seemed almost human.

How did the ants find their way back to the nest?

The ant hole leading into the underground nest was only slightly larger than the period at the end of this sentence. Surely, thought Turner, ants couldn't see the hole as clearly as he saw it from above.

As a young boy, Charles was always asking questions about nature. He wondered how and why an animal acts the way it does. He was especially interested in the small animals crawling and flying about. Constantly, he asked his teachers questions about the small creatures he saw.

Then, one day, his teacher replied, "If you want to know all of those things about them, why don't you go and find out for yourself?" Charles Turner answered, "I will."

Charles Turner spent a lifetime searching for answers to his many questions about animal behavior. In doing so, he made discoveries about the behavior of bees, moths, ants, cockroaches, and other insects, and he became one of the great scientists of the twentieth century.

Between 1892 and 1923, Charles H. Turner had 49 scientific articles accepted for publication. These articles, reporting his experiments, discoveries, and ideas about animal behavior, appeared in the leading scientific journals of his time, such as the *Biological Bulletin*, the *Journal of Comparative Neurology*, the *Zoological Bulletin*, the *Journal of Animal Behavior*, and the *Psychological Bulletin*.

Charles Turner's scientific research appeared in such articles as "Psychological Notes on the Gallery Spider," "The Habits of Mound-Building Ants," "Behavior of the Parasitic Bee," "The Hunting Habits of an American Sand Wasp," and "Do Ants Form Practical Judgment?"

Both the quality and quantity of Dr. Turner's work were impressive. His scientific research was studied and highly regarded by other animal investigators in America and Europe. Dozens of quotations from Turner's articles were cited in such important books on animal behavior as *Wheeler's Ant Book*, *The Animal Mind* (by Washburn), *Mind in Animals* (by Smith), and *The Psychic Life of Insects* (by Bouvier, a French scientist).

Here is a section taken from *The Animal Mind*:

> Recently, C. H. Turner has come to the conclusion that ants are not guided "slavishly" or reflexly by the odor of their tracks in finding their way to and from the nest. He made a small cardboard stage from which an inclined cardboard bridge led down to the artificial ant nest. Ants and pupae were placed on the stage. After the ants had, through random movements, learned the way down the incline, a second incline was placed so as to lead from the opposite side of the stage to the nest. No ants went down this way.
>
> The inclines were then exchanged so that the one bearing the scent of the ant's footprints was on the opposite side and the unscented incline in the old place; the ants continued to go down in the old place. . . . [Turner] confirms the observation that the pathways to and from the nest are different, but does not find that even a single ant follows her own footsteps in both directions. The direction of the light, not the smell, is the ruling factor in pathfinding, according to Turner.

In the animal behavior literature cf France, a certain characteristic ant movement was given the name of its discoverer, Dr. Turner. The movement was called "Turner's circling." It refers to a peculiar turning movement taken by some ants as they find their way home to a nest, a movement observed and described by Dr. Turner.

A Different Path

Charles H. Turner was born in 1867 in Cincinnati, Ohio, where he attended elementary school and graduated from high school. His father was a church custodian; his mother was a practical nurse.

It has been reported that Turner's father was a keen thinker with an intense thirst for knowledge. He acquired a large home library of several hundred books. One of young Charles' earliest ambitions was to learn to read his father's books.

In 1891, Charles Turner earned a bachelor of science degree and in 1892, a master of science degree, both from the University of Cincinnati. He taught in the biological laboratories at the University of Cincinnati for a brief time before moving on to other positions.

Turner could have devoted all of his time and energy to scientific research. However, he chose a different path— teaching full-time. So he carried on his research when he wasn't in the classroom with his pupils. Although he did go on to earn a doctoral degree in science, Turner never held a teaching position at a large university with out-standing research facilities.

Turner was committed instead to the education of young African Americans. His commitment is perhaps best reflected in this letter he wrote to Booker T. Washington, head of Tuskegee Institute (now Tuskegee University), in Tuskegee, Alabama:

BIOLOGICAL LABORATORY
University of Cincinnati

April 29, 1893

Prof. Booker T. Washington,
Dear Sir:

I am a colored man and at present am teaching in the University of Cincinnati (white). I am anxious to get to work among my own people. I would like to obtain a position as Professor of Natural History. Miss A. G. Baldwin informed me that you might know of an opening. Enclosed you will find copies of two letters of recommendation, etc. I can furnish several such at any time. Hoping to hear from you I am

Very truly,
C. H. Turner

Turner went to Clark College in Atlanta, Georgia, in 1893, as a professor of biology. From then until 1907, he held several positions in education, from a high-school teacher and principal to a college instructor in science. During this time, Turner undertook various experiments on spiders, crayfish, ants, and other invertebrates (animals without backbones).

For his pioneering work and his original discoveries and contributions to the field of animal behavior, Turner was awarded a doctoral degree in 1907 from the University of Chicago. For an African American in the early 1900s, this was an outstanding achievement.

On June 5, 1906, a handwritten letter of application for a teaching position was received by the principal of Sumner High School in St. Louis, Missouri. The letter was signed, "C. H. Turner." With the letter came this statement from the minister of Turner's church: "Charles H. Turner is a member in good and regular standing, . . . a scientist by nature and training."

In November 1908, Dr. Charles H. Turner became a teacher of biology at Sumner High School. His starting salary was $1,080 per year. He moved his family from Georgia to Missouri.

In her later years, Dr. Turner's daughter recalled that she and her brothers grew up in a scientific atmosphere, both in Georgia and in St. Louis. The family was accustomed to living with many books and laboratory specimens of ants, bees, roaches, snakes, and other creatures. These things kept his children interested in and curious about animal life and behavior.

"My father, to us, was just a plain, kind man who instilled in us those qualities that would make for the simple, successful life," Turner's daughter observed.

"Inorganic, Not Living Matter"

As a new teacher at Sumner High School in 1908, Dr. Turner had taken the place of the previous biology teacher, Mr. Clark. Some of the students in the senior class were curious to get a look at Mr. Clark's replacement, so a small group of them flocked to Dr. Turner's room to study.

Not knowing this new teacher's name, the class president decided he would ask. Dr. Turner then erased some writing from the chalkboard and wrote his name. The class president read aloud, "Dr. C. H. Turner, inorganic, not living matter." This, of course, brought laughter from the students. Dr. Turner smiled. The last phrase—"inorganic, not living matter"—was some writing that Turner had not erased from the chalkboard.

Turner taught biology at Sumner High School from 1908 until the time of his death in 1923. His lectures and courses were far from being non-living and inorganic. His students were impressed by the wealth of live animals and plants that he collected for study and experimentation. He acquired the most modern scientific instruments for his students. His lessons frequently required the use of microscopes. He clarified his lectures using colored chalk to draw exciting illustrations on the board, often using both hands at the same time.

Turner was a completely dedicated teacher. The welfare and development of his students was always foremost in his mind. Whenever he was not out alone in the field observing and experimenting, he would be out there with his students. He would take them on long hikes through the woods, stimulating in them a curiosity about nature and a reverence for life. He lifted his students into other worlds as they looked at nature through his eyes and mind. He translated the "coos" of pigeon talk into expressions of love, home planning, and family life. It seemed as if Dr. Turner really understood the language of birds.

Dr. Turner was an outstanding research scientist. He was also a committed and inspiring teacher. He brought a wealth of firsthand information about the behavior of living things to his classroom talks. His information was based on the research that he carried out in his spare time during the school year and during the summer months when insects and other living creatures were flourishing.

The notes below are excerpts taken from the notebook kept by Julia Davis, a student of Turner's in 1909:

ANTS

If you dig in an ant city when all kinds are present you will find several kinds.

Bachelor ants or drones are ants that are quite graceful, having two pairs of wings. They are more or less slender in shape and are the laziest ants known and are stupid; they never work but are always loafing up and down the city, and if they stray from home, there is no way for them to get back unless they are carried by another ant.

The young maiden or queen ant has two pairs of wings and is usually larger than the male but is not lazy like the male. She can do any kind of work. Only once in the life of the ant can the maiden fly or use her wings, and that is on her bridal tour.

That night or soon after the wedding, the bachelor ant dies. After the death of the bachelor ant, the widow comes to the surface of the ground and breaks off her wings. She has no more use for them since she never marries again.

Workers are old maid ants. They never marry. They are born from eggs laid by a mother ant. They hatch into a baby maiden ant without arms, legs, wings, antennae, or eyes. They must be washed, fed, and carried out to air by the mother ant. Everything must be done for them. At one point in its development, [the worker ant] stops eating and begins to spin a thread-like cocoon. Once wrapped in the cocoon, it grows into an adult.

HABITS OF ANTS

The toilet habits of ants are especially commendable. They are very clean. They clean themselves and their friends. On their appendages they have a comb and brush. The jaws are used to clean with also. Ants always have a dump pile where all undesired or refuse matter is placed. This dump pile is also their graveyard.

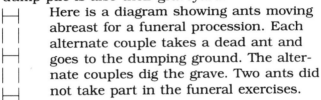 Here is a diagram showing ants moving abreast for a funeral procession. Each alternate couple takes a dead ant and goes to the dumping ground. The alternate couples dig the grave. Two ants did not take part in the funeral exercises.

BEHAVIOR OF BEES

Homing of Bees—Dr. Turner's experiment on mining bees. One morning on his way to school, Dr. Turner noticed a hole in the earth. Next to the hole was a bottle cap. A bee passed by and dropped into the hole. The bee came out of the hole and flew away, but she returned in about 20 minutes. The bee was collecting pollen from flowers in the field and storing it in an underground burrow. While the bee was afield, Dr. Turner made a hole in the earth with a stick and placed the bottle cap next to the hole he made.

When the bee returned from the field, the new hole was entered, but the bee came out immediately. She circled around and found her own hole and dropped into it. She soon came out again and was gone for 30 minutes. Dr. Turner made several more holes with the stick and placed bottle caps beside each hole. When the bee returned, she was confused. She could not find the right hole. The bee found her own hole only after hunting around and entering the wrong holes and finding they were not her home. These experiments showed that the bee relied on memory of the surroundings around the hole to find its home. . . .

Bees have the ability to tell time. In 1907, three times a day from 7-9, 12-2, and 5-7, the table was set with jam in dishes. The bees appeared at the table at all three meals. Then Dr. Turner put jam out only at breakfast daily. They still came to each meal but found no jam at noon and night. Soon they stopped coming. This shows they have some idea of time.

Dr. Turner was an unusual scientist. To find the truth about why and how animals behave as they do and to share his observations and discoveries with his students was of the greatest importance to him. He believed that the best possible way in which his discoveries could be used was to enrich the lives of young boys and girls.

Once, during an after-class conversation, one of Dr. Turner's students asked him why he chose to teach in a high school when he had been offered a professorship at the University of Chicago. This was at a time when few blacks were even admitted to large universities, much less offered positions as college instructors.

Dr. Turner's reply to his student's query revealed his deep commitment to other African Americans as well as to scientific research. "I feel that I am needed here and can do so much more for my people," he said.

After the death of Charles Turner, the St. Louis Board of Education erected a school for physically disabled black children and named it the Charles H. Turner School. In 1954, the school was converted to one for the seventh and eighth grades. Today, the Turner Middle School stands in memory of one of the city's greatest teachers and one of the country's outstanding scientists.

Colored Disks and Other Contraptions

Although Dr. Charles H. Turner was a biology teacher for most of his life, he was best known among scientists for his research work. He was known by the 50 research papers he had published on such subjects as neurology, invertebrate ecology, and animal behavior. In addition to research reports, Turner was asked to write reviews of the literature on comparative psychology in the *Psychological Bulletin* and in the *Journal of Animal Behavior*.

The science of animal behavior deals with the actions of single animals and animals in groups. This is not an easy thing to study. The heart of this science is twofold: describing what an animal does and then deciding if the action is important.

In studying animal behavior, a careful scientist must approach the subject with an open mind in deciding which movements or actions to record. Dr. Turner's most productive work was done in his many series of investigations into the behavior of insects.

Charles Turner spent much time thinking about his experimental method before he went into the field. He built ingenious devices to help him solve the problems of animal behavior. By using the apparatus shown on the following page, for example, Turner discovered that light rays were a larger factor than had previously been thought in helping ants to find their way home.

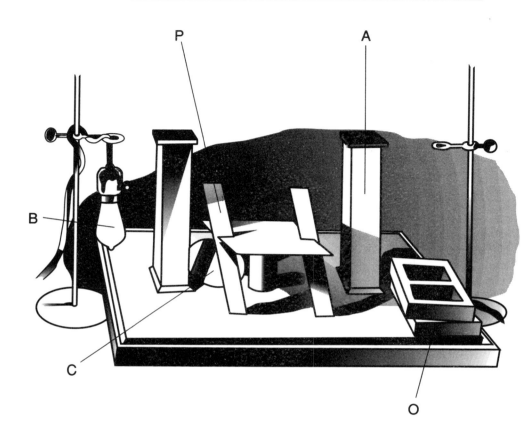

The stage, or platform, in the center of the apparatus was made of cardboard. By using a narrow inclined plane (P), Dr. Turner could connect the stage to a nest (O) of ants. To the right and left of the stage were electric lights (B). The lights were arranged so that when the light on one side was burning, the other automatically shut off. The lights were separated from the stage by heat filters (A). A mirror (C) was used for viewing ants crawling on the lower side of the inclined plane.

Dr. Turner placed a number of ants with their eggs, larvae, and pupae upon the stage. He switched on the light on the right side of the stage. Soon, a procession of ants was passing between the nest and the stage along the inclined plane on the right side. Then, Dr. Turner attached a second plane to the left side of the stage. He now had one incline on the side where the light was shining and another on the opposite side. The ants continued to travel along the pathway on the right.

After the ants had been using the lighted right side for several hours, Turner switched off the light on the right and turned on the light on the left. "Immediately a remarkable change occurred," said Dr. Turner. "The ants acted as though they were in a panic. They seemed lost."

Within an hour, the ants were using the plane on the left side to enter and leave the stage. Turner interpreted this result by noting that "light is a factor in guiding these ants home."

Turner was interested in comparing the method used by the burrowing bees to find their way home with the homing methods used by ants and wasps. At the time, some scientists believed that bees were guided by sun rays and wind. The bee homing experiments were carried out in a deserted garden. They were performed upon a bee that occupied a burrow all to itself. Turner explained how he determined how many bees occupied a burrow:

> I would plug the opening [entrance to the burrow] and then observe it carefully for an hour or longer. The bees, on returning, would circle about the nest. After a while,

they would usually try to dig around the plug. By counting the bees that appeared and tarried, it was easy to determine how many bees were occupying the burrow. When the required information was obtained, the plug was removed.

The burrow was situated in a small barren spot and surrounded by a few blades of grass partially covering the opening. Before the first three experiments were done, Dr. Turner had observed a bee arrive at 9 35 A.M. and enter the burrow. At 9:37 A.M., it departed again for the field. The bee was making 20-minute trips to flowers in the field for pollen, which it was storing in the burrow.

In his work on the homing of burrowing bees, Dr. Turner spent from 5 to 10 hours a day during the month of August 1908 studying these insects in the field. This made it possible for Turner to conduct several series of experiments. This is how Turner described some of the 20 experiments he carried out during the summer:

Experiment 1:

> While the bee was afield, a rectangular piece of white paper, 12 cm. by 8 cm., in the center of which was a hole 13 mm. in diameter, was so adjusted over the nest as to have the hole in the paper coincide with the opening of the burrow.

At 9:55 A.M., the bee arrived with its burden of pollen. Instead of entering the nest, it circled around and around. It then hovered momentarily over the white rectangle and then described yet wider circles in the air. At 9:57 A.M., two minutes after its return from the field, the bee entered the nest. On again departing for the field, at 10:00 A.M., the bee hovered a while above the paper that surrounded the nest; after making several turns of a [spiral] curve, flew away.

Experiment 2:

The same conditions as in Experiment 1.

At 10:20 A.M., the bee arrived from its trip, hovered for less than half a minute and then dropped into the nest. At 10:24 A.M., the bee departed, without stopping to explore the surroundings of the nest.

Experiment 3:

About four inches to the east of the nest opening, a hole was made in the ground. Over this hole was placed the piece of white paper, with the hole in the center, which was adjusted over the nest in Experiment 2.

A piece of watermelon rind, with a 13 mm. hole in the center, was so adjusted over the nest as to have the hole in the rind coincide with the opening of the burrow. One-half of the rind was brown, the other half yellowish-green; the line dividing these two colors bisected the hole in the center of the rind.

At 10:47 A.M., the bee arrived with its burden of pollen. It hovered above the watermelon rind for a moment, then circled about the place. At 10:48 A.M., after a search of one minute, the bee entered the nest. On leaving the nest at 10:59 A.M., the bee examined carefully the surroundings before departing.

Experiment 4:

While the bee was afield, the piece of watermelon rind was removed and a rectangular piece of white paper, 8 cm. long and 5 cm. wide, was arched over the nest in such a way as to form a tent 6 cm. high, the east and west ends of which were open. The rectangular piece of white paper, with the hole in the center, which was left in the same position as in Experiment 3, was situated just in front of the eastern opening of the tent.

When the bee arrived, at 11:15 A.M., it circled about for two minutes (until 11:17 A.M.) and then dropped into the hole over which the rectangular piece of paper, with the hole in its center, had been adjusted. It emerged at once and, after circling about for a short time, re-entered the hole. It emerged immediately. Finally at 11:18 A.M., three minutes after arriving on the spot, the bee entered the tent through the eastern opening and dropped into the burrow. On emerging from the nest at 11:31 A.M. the bee hovered a moment inside of the tent. It then passed out of the east opening and hovered for a few seconds above the tent. Then, keeping close to the top of the grass, it flew about for a while in a [spiral] curve and then flew away to the field.

As a result of these experiments, Turner concluded that burrowing bees are guided by memory in finding their way home. According to Turner, bees examine carefully the neighborhood of their nests for the purpose of forming "memory pictures" of the topography (the surface of the land) around the burrow. Any change in the topography seemed to confuse the bees upon returning to find the entrance to their homes.

Another question that Dr. Turner wanted to answer was this: What attracts insects to flowers—the sweet odor or the color of the flowers? For many years, scientists had been trying to learn if bees could see colors. They wanted to know if colors guided the bees to flowers. The results of the various experiments were often contradictory.

During the summer of 1910, Dr. Turner carried out some experiments in O'Fallon Park in St. Louis. Using his ever ingenious methods, he designed tests with colored disks of paper and boxes that were filled with honey. He found that odors alone did not lead bees to flowers. Based on his findings, Turner believed that bees responded to colors in many ways and, furthermore, that they were capable of recognizing colors at a great distance.

At the end of a research article titled "Experiments on Color-Vision of the Honey Bee," published by the Marine Biological Laboratory at Woods Hole, Massachusetts, Dr. Turner came to the following conclusion:

> These experiments prove that, to the bee, my colored disks, my colored cornucopias, and my colored boxes were something more than mere sensations. . . . Those strange red things had come to mean "honey-bearers," and those strange green things and strange blue things had come to mean "not honey-bearers." Hence, whenever the bees saw the red things, they made the appropriate movements for securing the honey, and when they saw the blue things or the green things, they passed on.

In 1910, another scientist, J. H. Lovell, published an article resulting from his own research with bees. Lovell's article was titled "The Color Sense of the Honey Bee: Can Bees Distinguish Colors?" Dr. Lovell used an experimental method that was quite different from Dr. Turner's, yet Lovell's results led him to form the same conclusions.

Charles Turner was not content with discovering that bees were capable of sensing colors. A year later, Turner carried out a series of experiments proving that bees are able to distinguish between different patterns, too.

Once again, Turner used ingeniously devised paper boxes with various color markings. The paper boxes served as artificial flowers. His method was to encourage a few bees to learn that they could collect honey more easily from artificial flowers of a certain color pattern than they could from real flowers. After the bees had learned this, Dr. Turner tried to find out if the bees could select the artificial flowers with this particular color pattern from a number of different color patterns.

The result of Turner's investigation was the discovery that bees can, in fact, distinguish color patterns. Turner believed that this ability was of value to bees in recognizing plants that yield honey.

The Power of Observation

All of Dr. Turner's work did not involve experimentation. Sometimes, he would just sit for hours and observe the actions of insects. The pit-making ant-lion, a marvel of the insect world, was one of his favorite insects to study.

Turner described in detail the ant-lion's method of excavating a pit in the ground. When the pit was complete, it served as a trap for other insects. He explained the method that the creature used in capturing prey, which it sucked dry with its hollow jaws.

With painstaking experiments, Dr. Turner worked out the details of this insect's ability to "play possum." He concluded that the ant-lion suddenly "played dead" as its instinctive way of reacting when startled. When the ant-lion lies motionless for prolonged periods of time, Turner reported, "it is really not feigning death at all, and requires no self-command. It is simply terror paralysis which has become so useful that it has become hereditary."

Dr. Turner also did some important research on the common cockroach. In a paper entitled "Behavior of the Common Roach on an Open Maze," he found that a roach could be taught within a day to run a maze. The roach learned by trial and error but, in doing so, also used its senses to find its way through the maze.

In another study, Dr. Turner worked with roaches that were nocturnal. These insects shunned the light. But Turner trained them to reverse their lifelong habit and to avoid the dark instead. This was done by teaching them to avoid certain dark places. Every time the cockroach approached one of these dark places, it would receive an electric shock from a device made by Dr. Turner. Turner found that male roaches seemed to learn more quickly than the females and that young roaches were quicker to learn than adult roaches.

During Dr. Turner's time, most naturalists believed that insects could hear. But this had never been proved experimentally. Scientists thought that since insects can produce sounds, then other members of the species must be able to hear them. Dr. Turner proved that a certain kind of moth could not only hear sounds, but also sounds of various pitches. He demonstrated this with an organ pipe and a whistle. Moreover, he discovered that a species that at first responds only to a high pitch on the whistle can be taught to respond to low tones when the low tones mean danger to the insect.

Both scientists and students of nature were grateful for the many research contributions of Charles Turner.

A Better Quality of Life

The handicaps under which Charles Turner's work was accomplished were many, but they were bravely met. One of these was the limitation of a small salary, out of which Turner had to purchase his scientific equipment, materials, and books for research. He did not have the use of elaborate research laboratories and the kind of modern facilities available to many professional scientists. In his studies, Turner did not venture on lengthy and costly trips to faraway places. He had the ability to take the material that was near at hand and make the most of it.

Charles Turner's interests were not solely scientific. Found among his unfinished papers were several chapters of a novel, a number of chapters of a book of nature stories for children, and the manuscript for a book of poems.

Turner also spent time and energy working for civil rights and a better quality of life for the African-American people in St. Louis. He pioneered the development of social service work among black people there. When Turner died in 1923, not only did science lose one of its most thorough and inventive students, but black people lost a productive advocate for civil rights.

On May 25, 1923, a memorial service for Dr. Charles H. Turner was held in the auditorium of Sumner High School in St. Louis. Many people spoke of Dr. Turner that day. One of the speakers was A. G. Pohlman, who came to represent the Academy of Science of St. Louis. It is fitting to close this chapter with Pohlman's moving words.

Charles Henry Turner

An Appreciation

It has been said that the size of a man may be measured in terms of his influence for good and for the betterment of his fellow man. But just as the striving to attain is more important to us than the desired thing itself, so we tend to look abroad for a truly great man when, forsooth, he walks in our very midst.

We are very likely to think of the great man as one who has acquired a vast amount of money, or as one who has gained social prominence, or as one whose opinion on public questions is eagerly sought. Many people mistake notoriety for fame, confuse the word politician for states- man, take for granted that well-known is the equivalent for great. Were not these historians so overcome with the pomp and the splendor of a Pilate that they quite forgot to men- tion the humble Carpenter of Nazareth? It may be well to consider some of the features which go to make up the truly great man, that those of us who have sought afar shall recognize a brother who perhaps at this moment is touching elbows with us.

The first essential in the great man is a devotion to work. Some of us envy the well-known man who toils but little and therein we cater to our own ambitions of las- situde. But no man is great unless he rises above the petty inconveniences of his surroundings. No man is strong un- less he meets the competition about him.

Devotion to work means exactly what it says. It does not mean devotion to methods. It does not imply a certain number of hours a day. It does not suggest a contentment with the doing of a daily stint in a manner which calls for neither commendation nor criticism.

Devotion to work means work because one must work, and faced by such a spirit, seemingly insurmountable obstacles are swept away along with trivial factors of birth and race and station.

But work itself is not enough. The second ingredient in our strength of character is unselfishness: the desire to share the joys and sorrows of life with others, the accomplishment of the friendly act for its own sake; the appreciation of a bond of proper sympathy of man for man. The man who works for unselfish devotion ever searches for that which shall bring his neighbor to a higher level of doing and thinking and living. A great man must indeed be unselfish and take pride in the merit which his talent may lend others.

And in the search for truth, even in the little things of life, our great man interprets that which he finds and is ever threading the beads of fact into some pattern of a worldly philosophy. Faithfulness to truth is, after all, a faithfulness to the little things, and our great man achieves merit in his respect for that which is known and that which is unknown. Because of his consciousness of his own limitations and because of his respect for truth, the great man is humble.

We have been misinformed in our ideas of great men. We have been misled into looking for magnificence and for vainglorious trappings in which our fancy would clothe an important person. Indeed the humble simplicity of the truly great man disarms us quite completely, and we crane the neck to overlook exactly that which we seek.

It is for you who knew Dr. Turner to satisfy yourself that here indeed was a great man. It is for you to determine in your own hearts if this man possessed the strength of character, the devotion to work, the faithfulness to ideals, the respect for truth, and the unselfishness in sharing that which he possessed. Was he indeed the humble man of science who might well be taken into the fold of the most highly esteemed?

You have answered this question yourselves. It will not be given to many of us that men and women and little children shall gather together after we are gone to pay tribute to our memory. It is a privilege to appear before you as a representative of the Academy of Science, an organization of which Dr. Turner was not only a member but also a councilor. Let each one of you cherish the memory of Dr. Turner, who left behind him the priceless heritage of devoted service that those who knew him and worked with him cannot help but have been the better and the stronger through his contact.

Permit me, in the name of the Academy of Science, to pay our respect not only to Turner the Scientist, but also to Turner the Man.

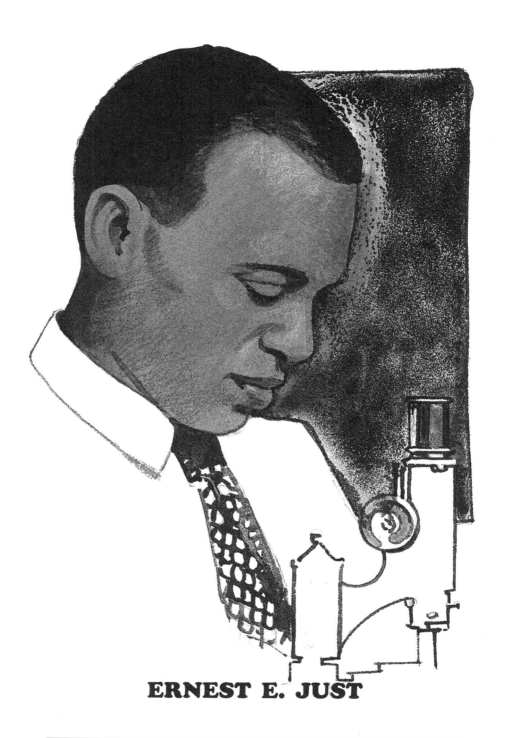

ERNEST E. JUST

3

On the evening of February 12, 1915, the governor of the state of New York stood on the stage at the Ethical Culture Hall in New York City. In his hand was a gold medal, the Spingarn Medal, to be awarded for the first time. The medal was to go "to the man or woman of African descent and American citizenship who shall have made the highest achievement during the preceding year or years in any honorable field of human endeavor."

On the stage behind the governor sat his staff and the officials of the National Association for the Advancement of Colored People (NAACP), the organization giving the medal. Each year (except one) since 1915, the NAACP has presented this award. In recent years, the medal has been given to such people as Jesse Jackson, Bill Cosby, Lena Horne, and Colin Powell.

The man who was to receive the first Spingarn Medal was not a social reformer. He had not made any great speeches about equality for African Americans. He had not led any successful protest movements for the civil rights of his people.

Ernest E. Just was being recognized for his work as a scientist. He had been carrying out pioneering investigations on the nature of animal cells. Ernest Just was a brilliant investigator of the living cell, especially the egg cells of marine animals. He had earned the reputation of being a "scientist's scientist."

Dr. Charles R. Drew, a prominent medical scientist, called Ernest Just "a biologist of unusual skill and the greatest of our original thinkers in the field."

Everyone was glad to be at the Ethical Culture Hall that evening, everyone except Ernest E. Just.

He wished that he could have been working in his laboratory, teaching a group of students, or at home reading—anywhere but on a stage in front of an audience of people who were listening to speeches praising him. Dr. Just hated publicity. This was an embarrassing evening for the young scientist. In fact, he had tried to prevent it.

Dr. Just had written to the officials of the NAACP to say that he was disturbed about being the winner of the award. In a letter to the secretary of the NAACP, he wrote that he was not interested in publicity:

> My contributions have been meager. It rather upsets me to learn that I am expected to be present at the award ceremony, doubtless in the presence of a large audience. I feel deeply that I ought not court publicity, since courtship ought to be incompatible with scientific endeavor.

But despite Just's modesty and his dislike for the attention being given his work as a scientist, the medal could not be denied him.

When Dr. Ernest Just stepped forward to receive the Spingarn Medal from the governor, he whispered a polite thank-you and shrank back into his seat. He appreciated the honor, and it filled him with an even greater sense of determination to solve the mysteries of life in his work as a research biologist.

Indeed, Just did go on to discover some of the answers he sought. He also went on to work and study with some of the greatest minds in twentieth-century biology at one of the most famous research laboratories in the United States and other famous laboratories in Germany, France, and Italy.

In 35 years of productive research, Ernest Just added new information and ideas about the structure and workings of the living cell. And although Just was modest and quiet about his work, he was not afraid to challenge the theories of some of the great biologists of the time.

In 1916, Ernest E. Just received his doctoral degree from the University of Chicago for his studies of animal reproduction. In later years, other distinguished biologists voted that a star be placed by his name in *American Men of Science*.

The star indicated that his fellow scientists thought of him as a leader in the field of biological science. During his lifetime, Dr. Just published two books—*Basic Methods for Experiments on Eggs of Marine Animals* and *The Biology of the Cell Surface*—and more than 60 papers describing his experiments.

In the 1920s and 1930s, Dr. Ernest Just probably knew more about the egg cells of marine animals and their development into new life than any other biologist.

The cell is the basic living part of all living things. Live cells contain a complex mixture of elements and compounds. The interaction of the hundreds of substances within cells produces living material as we know it.

Humans and most animals that you are familiar with begin life as single cells. This original cell comes from the union of two specialized cells, one from each of the parents of the new animal. When a sperm cell from the father meets an egg cell from the mother and joins with it to form one cell, a new life begins. The joining of a sperm and an egg cell is called fertilization. The fertilized egg then begins to divide into more cells and is known as an embryo. Eventually, after thousands of cell divisions, the embryo develops into a fully grown animal made up of millions and millions of cells.

One of the frontiers of science today is the creation of some substances found in cells. It is only because of the pioneering work of scientists like Dr. Just that today's scientists are getting closer to knowing how to create life in a test tube.

As science advances, it builds on the knowledge left by the great thinkers of the past. Ernest Just was one of the first scientists to unlock the secrets of cell reproduction and to present new theories of cell life.

In 1915, when he became the first Spingarn medalist, Ernest Just was only 32 years old. It was only eight years before that he had graduated from Dartmouth College.

Preparing for His Life's Work

Dartmouth College, in Hanover, New Hampshire, is far away from Charleston, South Carolina, the southern city in which Ernest Just was born in 1883. His father, a builder of wharves, died when Ernest was four years old. His mother was a teacher, and she guided her son's early childhood education.

At 17, after finishing his public schooling at a school for black students in Orangeburg, South Carolina, Just left his birthplace and headed north for a better education.

Ernest Just spent his first summer away from home working in New York. He earned enough money to take him even farther north, to the Kimball Academy in New Hampshire. Kimball Academy was a four-year school that prepared boys for college. At Kimball, Ernest Just was placed in the lowest class despite the fact that he had spent six years in school in Orangeburg. His schooling in South Carolina really had not prepared Just for college, so four more years of high school lay ahead. But a college education remained foremost in his mind. He worked hard at his studies and finished four years' work at Kimball in three years.

Just was an excellent student and made a brilliant academic record. His teachers at Kimball recommended that he go to Dartmouth College, not far from Kimball. With scholarship aid and loans, he was able to begin his college studies at Dartmouth.

At Dartmouth, Just was interested in only one thing—preparing himself for his life's work. At first, college life was not what he thought it would be. During his freshman year, he often thought that perhaps he was in the wrong place. It seemed that the only thing anyone at Dartmouth ever talked about or cared about was football. The rivalry between Dartmouth and Harvard University gripped the campus. A freshman who was not out at every game rooting for the team was frowned upon.

As his sophomore year began, the success of the football team still seemed more important to most students than scholarship. This disappointed Just. He felt that he was not getting the kind of intellectual stimulation that he had expected from discussions with other students. Lonely and discouraged, he was ready to leave Dartmouth when he began his first science course—biology.

In this course, he read about one of the mysteries of science—the development of the animal egg. This topic fascinated him, and biology became his true love, as football had become for so many other students.

Ernest Just took every course in biology offered at Dartmouth. His work was considered to be outstanding. During his senior year, Just spent a good deal of his time on a research problem concerning the development and growth of egg cells.

In June 1907, Ernest Just graduated from Dartmouth with a degree in zoology. He was the only student in his class to graduate with highest honors. The deep interest that he had acquired in the development of the egg was to stay with him for the rest of his life.

Ernest Just went directly from Dartmouth to teach at Howard University in Washington, D.C., then and now a predominantly black university. In 1912, he became head of the Department of Zoology at Howard, a position he held until his death in 1941. Dr. Just was also on the faculty of the Howard University Medical School as a professor and head of the Department of Physiology.

The work of Ernest Just toward improving medical education at Howard and other medical schools for black students was extremely effective. At the same time, his research studies into the nature of living cells began to attract the attention of prominent biologists throughout the world.

Although Just was dedicated to his teaching and his work at Howard, he left Washington each summer to carry on his research at the Marine Biological Laboratory at Woods Hole, on Cape Cod in Massachusetts. From 1909 to 1930, Just spent every summer except one in Woods Hole. The Marine Biological Laboratory there is a special place, famous in the history of biological science. It was there that Ernest Just carried out his greatest work in biological science.

Where Life Began

Almost all of the world's great biologists have spent some time at the Marine Biological Laboratory at Woods Hole. In the early part of this century, nearly every young biologist would either study at the laboratory or would study under people who had done so.

During the summer months, as they still do today, scientists from colleges and universities in this country and abroad gathered at the Marine Biological Laboratory to study the diverse and abundant marine life found in the surrounding waters. In 1909, Dr. Frank R. Lillie, a scientist from the University of Chicago, was one such researcher. Ernest Just was to become one of his students and, later, his collaborator and friend.

The Woods Hole laboratory was known as the place where students in the early stages of important research could be found during the summer. Some were destined to become great scientific leaders, like Just.

Young researchers always found special provisions for their laboratory needs at Woods Hole, and most of them came with their own professors. The discussions among students and professors have played an important part in scientific careers begun and fostered at Woods Hole.

It is only natural to wonder why a marine biological laboratory and the study of marine forms of life would be important to biologists investigating basic problems of the life sciences. There are two reasons for this.

First of all, the oceans have changed much less than the land's surface throughout the history of the Earth. Since the ocean environment has been so constant, there is reason to believe that the first living things, as we know them, probably originated in the ocean waters. The oceans contain forms of animal life never found on the continents, and these forms represent every major group of animals especially adapted to the ocean environment. The rapid development of zoology and botany during the late 1800s naturally led to the creation of marine research stations.

Second, as newer experimental methods began to be used in biology, it was discovered that marine specimens offered exceptional advantages for scientists investigating basic problems dealing with protoplasm, the living stuff inside cells. Seawater is very much like protoplasm. The fluids inside the bodies of most marine animals contain the same salts as the sea and in about the same proportions and concentrations.

Also, the eggs of many marine animals—such as sea urchins, starfish, and various worms—are deposited in enormous numbers into seawater. When these eggs are taken into the laboratory for study and experimentation, they can be cultivated in glass dishes.

Ernest Just began his graduate studies at the Marine Biological Laboratory at Woods Hole in 1909 by taking a course in marine invertebrates (sea animals without back-bones). During the summers of 1911 and 1912, Dr. Just assisted Frank Lillie in fertilization studies and the breeding habits of the sandworm (Nereis) and the sea urchin (Arbacia). His work was so good that by 1916 Just had completed six papers based on his work at Woods Hole during the summer months.

Each spring after 1916, when his classes ended at Howard, Dr. Just headed north to Woods Hole to study with the world's leading scientists. The stimulating environment of alert, critical minds at Woods Hole did much toward developing Just as an outstanding scientist. Dr. Just continued to work closely with Dr. Lillie, his first teacher at the Marine Biological Laboratory, and they soon became good friends.

Dr. Just would usually arrive at Woods Hole three to four weeks before the other scientists and would leave after most of the others had returned to their colleges at the summer's end. He would arrive early in order to work with the curator of the animal supply department and the animal collecting crew.

Together, they would carefully examine the marine animals that were to be used in Dr. Just's investigations during the summer months. Just insisted on having the best animal specimens possible to work with, and he knew that the collection methods affected the condition of the captured animals.

The eggs of marine animals, which were the center of Dr. Just's attention, live for only about 24 hours outside a female animal's body. Dr. Just needed fresh eggs for much of his work. Sandworms hatched from eggs found in waters near the laboratory would swarm together only during the part of the month when the moon was between its third-quarter and full phases. Attracted by the light of the moon, they would appear swimming near the surface of the water about an hour after sunset. So at this time, Dr. Just spent many evenings at the water's edge with a lantern, a net, and some collecting dishes.

Just would hold the lantern above the water and allow it to swing. The light from his lantern attracted the worms, which could readily be caught with a hand net.

The males would appear first, shedding their sperm cells into the water. Masses of these sperm cells looked like milky white clouds in the seawater. The females were attracted by the bright red color of the males, who whirled around the water surface in the area lit up by the lantern. The females would respond to the whirling motion of the males by shedding their eggs into the water. The worms shedding their reproductive cells were caught and placed in the same dishes. Then, or soon afterward, the eggs would be fertilized by the sperm cells.

Since fertilized and unfertilized egg cells did not live long, Dr. Just had to make his observations immediately. He would carry his dishes of worms and eggs back to his laboratory and work through the night studying the eggs under his microscope.

If Dr. Just wanted reproductive cells to study the next day, the male and female worms were kept in separate covered dishes overnight and placed in a seawater table with water flowing over them. To obtain the eggs the next morning, he placed a female worm in clean seawater and snipped the worm with sharp scissors. The eggs would pour forth quickly from the worm's body. The cut worm was removed immediately, and the eggs were washed in clean seawater.

The males were similarly washed in seawater and then dried with soft filter paper. Next, they were cut in half between the head and tail. This provided Dr. Just with bloodless, dry sperm cells. The sperm were mixed with a small amount of seawater; then, two crops of this sperm suspension were added to the eggs of one female. The mixing of the sperm and egg cells was done under a microscope. This allowed Dr. Just to study every detail of the sperm's entering the egg cell (fertilization) and the development of the egg that followed.

Questioning the Experts

In the early 1900s, scientists had shown that the eggs of some marine animals could actually develop without being fertilized by a sperm cell. The name given to this phenomenon is parthenogenesis. If an egg were made to develop by something the scientist did in the laboratory, the process was known as artificial parthenogenesis.

Full embryo development can be started in an egg (including frogs and rabbits) by a salt solution, electric shock, and other artificial agents. This was shown at the turn of this century by Jacques Loeb of the University of

Chicago and T. H. Morgan of Columbia University in the first demonstration of artificial parthenogenesis.

Jacques Loeb was considered to be a scientific leader. He was a well-known authority for his work in fertilization and especially artificial parthenogenesis. Loeb founded a famous theory of fertilization known as the lysin theory. This theory stated that two substances were needed for artificial parthenogenesis.

First, according to Loeb's theory, eggs must be treated with a chemical substance called butyric acid; then, the eggs must be treated with hypertonic seawater. (Hypertonic seawater has a higher concentration of salt than ordinary seawater.) Treatment with these two substances would cause eggs to develop into larvae. Further, Loeb found that if the hypertonic seawater were used before the butyric acid, the results would be the same. Loeb's theory lasted for about two decades.

In 1922, Dr. Just made an attack on Loeb's famous theory. Just presented evidence that hypertonic seawater alone would start development of the egg of the sea urchin.

During the summer of 1921, Dr. Just produced free-swimming larvae of sea urchins by allowing only hypertonic seawater to act on unfertilized eggs of this marine animal. The larvae that Just produced through artificial parthenogenesis looked no different from larvae developed from eggs that had been normally fertilized by sperm in the ocean.

This sample of Just's work with the sea urchin egg shows that scientific theories must always be questioned, that they must be altered when new evidence from new experiments is produced. Just had shown that hypertonic seawater alone could cause parthenogenesis.

In addition to being a skillful experimenter, Dr. Just also had a great and rather playful imagination. He was not afraid to explore new fields and problems that others might think ridiculous.

For example, he wondered if magnetism would affect the division of cells that followed egg fertilization. His few investigations into this area showed that magnetism did have some effect on cell division. In the late 1960s, some space scientists were interested in the same question. In one of the biosatellites that carried a variety of animals and plants into outer space, sea urchin eggs were also sent along. Scientists wanted to study the effects, if any, of the Earth's magnetic field and radiation on the activity of these cells.

Dr. Just was a quiet man most of the time, especially while working at his laboratory bench. He would work for many hours without saying a single word to those working around him. He and Dr. Lillie used to carry on a game to see who would say the least number of words during the day while working in the lab together.

One evening, during supper in the mess hall at the Marine Biological Laboratory, Lillie remarked to those who were sitting around the table, "Well, I beat Just today. I said only three words."

"Oh, no," replied Just, smiling. "I beat him today. I said only one."

Understanding What Is Normal

Dr. Just came to know more about normal eggs and the normal egg development of marine life than any other investigator at Woods Hole. Other scientists would frequently seek him out for his advice on working with eggs. He would never do an experiment unless he was absolutely sure that his eggs were normal, for only normal eggs would undergo normal development after fertilization.

Dr. Just was often critical of the work of scientists who did not know what normal development was or who were using eggs that were not normal to begin with in their experiments.

What was a normal egg to Dr. Just? And why was knowing about its development so important to him?

Just examined hundreds of eggs of different animals so that he would know and be able to recognize the normal development of their eggs in the laboratory after fertilization. This was a laborious task. But once he knew what normal laboratory development was, then he could better recognize abnormal development if it occurred.

Recognition of normal or abnormal egg development was important because of the kinds of experiments that Just carried out with eggs and fertilization. In his various experiments, he would try to find out the effects of such factors as water temperature, the salt concentration in seawater, ultraviolet light, magnetism, and evaporation of seawater on fertilization and subsequent egg development. These factors are called experimental variables.

Before Dr. Just set up or began an experiment, he would follow the development of the egg in the laboratory to be sure it was normal. Since a fertilized egg changes so quickly and dramatically during the first 24 hours, Just constantly had to watch the eggs through his microscope. If the egg or its development were not normal during the first hours after fertilization, then he could not be sure that any changes he later observed in the developing egg were caused by the experimental factor.

In order to start with normal eggs and have normal egg development in the laboratory, the laboratory conditions for the eggs must be exactly like the natural sea-water conditions in the oceans. Over a period of years, Just learned how to maintain natural conditions for eggs and how to handle the eggs in the laboratory so that they wouldn't be harmed in any way that would affect their development before he used them. Because Just was so meticulous about starting with normal eggs, his experiments were highly productive and successful.

Putting It Down on Paper

In the 1800s and early 1900s, much valuable and time-saving research information had been lost because it passed from scientist to scientist only by word of mouth. Just's fellow scientists urged him to make his knowledge of methods for successful experiments with marine eggs available to scientists at Woods Hole and others working in laboratories around the country. In order to preserve his knowledge of methods of working with marine eggs for future generations of scientists, Dr. Just wrote his first book. It was called *Basic Methods for Experiments on Eggs of Marine Animals.* This book has been so important and useful over the years to researchers that it was revised and updated in 1957 by scientists working at Woods Hole.

In this book, Dr. Just described methods for handling the eggs and sperm cells of 28 different kinds of marine animals in the laboratory. Just included his techniques for preparing glass slides for viewing reproductive cells under a microscope. He also discussed such variables as glassware, the use of seawater, and temperature—factors that affect the nature of animals and eggs.

Just's book illustrates how careful his preparations for experimentation were. Here are some of the things that Dr. Just learned from his years of research experience in the laboratory:

On Cleanliness: The first rule to be observed by the experimenter in egg development is that of scrupulous cleanliness. Contamination in all forms must be avoided. It represents a serious source of error. *Be at great pains to insure the absolute cleanliness of every utensil used.* This precaution is as important as any taken against accidental contamination during the actual experimental work.

On Glassware: Ordinarily one uses an acid cleaner. After its use, the glassware should be washed in running water until the most delicate test for acid gives no reaction. Soap and soap powders, if not thoroughly removed, will modify experimental results when mixed with sea-water. I find that Bon Ami is superior to soap and soap powders because it is easily removed. It leaves the glassware bright and clear. After removing the dried Bon Ami with dry towels, the glassware is rinsed in running water for several minutes. *The glassware is then stacked upright, and never upside down for fear of chance contamination,* on dry linen towels. . . . I never use laboratory towels for drying glassware without having previously washed them in running water. . . .

On Temperature: It is well to record both the room temperature and that of sea-water containing eggs. One should have available two standardized thermometers. . . . The room temperature should be taken always in the same place in the room which should be protected against sunshine. The dishes containing the eggs, the temperature of which is taken, should be similarly placed and protected.

In view of the fact that change in temperature is a very important experimental means, the worker should keep careful record of the temperature at which he conducts his experiments. . . .

Further, unless eggs are normally found in sea-water of low temperature, *they should never be kept in the cold* except for the expressed purpose of investigating the effect of low temperature on an egg whose normal habitat is [at a] higher [temperature]. I know of many investigators who have kept their animals on ice overnight in order to delay the shedding of eggs. This practice, I think, cannot be too severely condemned.

The Use of Sea-Water: Dishes containing eggs should always be protected against evaporation, because this makes the sea-water hypertonic and hypertonic sea-water is itself an experimental method. (Hypertonic sea-water is sea-water with a higher concentration of salt than usual.) More than once results have been reported as due to an experimental treatment which actually were brought about by the evaporation of the sea-water containing eggs. Therefore, the dishes should be covered. On warm days it is well to keep such dishes on the live table in running sea-water. . . . Dishes containing eggs should, of course, be protected against direct sunlight.

The Collection of Eggs: Many animals, especially those living at great depths of the sea, cannot with profit be collected by the scientist himself. Here he must depend upon the collecting staff. However excellent the apparatus for the collecting may be, the factor of prime importance is the collectors. If these be inefficient or untrustworthy, the experimenter will suffer because of the bad condition of the animals furnished him. . . . Whenever the experimenter in egg development is dependent upon others for the collecting of breeding animals or of eggs, he must be confident that the collecting is properly accomplished. He should be sure that he has freshly collected organisms or cells; if these be aged, he has now to reckon with age as an additional complicating factor in his experiments.

Just felt very strongly about these and other rules that he set down about working with marine animals and their eggs. He looked most unfavorably on scientists who claimed results from their experiments but did not follow these simple rules.

"An experiment," Ernest Just wrote, "should never in the least way be clouded by uncertainty concerning the normal process."

In the late 1920s, Frank Lillie, himself an authority on fertilization (and perhaps Just's closest colleague), gave this glowing evaluation of his former student:

In the 20 summer sessions that Ernest Just spent at the Marine Biological Laboratory at Woods Hole, he became more widely acquainted with the embryological resources of the marine animals than probably any other person, and he learned to handle the material with skill and understanding. In consequence, he was in great demand, especially by physiologists who knew physics and chemistry better than biology, for advice and assistance which he rendered generously. When he withdrew from Woods Hole to work in European laboratories, his loss to the scientific community was deeply felt.

Greater Opportunity

As a scientist, Dr. Ernest Just was well respected. He was able, versatile, and productive. Just received many awards and grants to support his research projects. He was a member of the corporation of the Marine Biological Laboratory and was on the editorial board of the *Biological Bulletin*, the official research journal of the laboratory at Woods Hole.

Just's articles appeared in several European scientific journals as well as the *Biological Bulletin*. He was elected vice president of the American Society of Zoologists.

As a man, however, Ernest Just was frustrated and embittered. For even with his intelligence, insight, and perseverance, he found the walls of racial prejudice and discrimination in America too high to climb. He felt that, despite his ability and achievement, he was not completely accepted at Woods Hole because he was a black man. He felt that limitations were placed upon his career because of his race.

In fact, Just would not encourage other young black students to try for a career as a research biologist. Though he taught the biological sciences at Howard University during most of his adult life, he attempted to steer most of his students into careers as doctors rather than to have them follow in his footsteps. His students in pure biology from 1907 to 1941 were very few.

By 1930, Dr. Just still had much uncompleted work to do. He felt a need for the greater opportunity that he could find in the research facilities of foreign laboratories.

Through no fault of its own, Howard University did not have the facilities to give full opportunity to Just's goals and ambitions. This institution had cooperated fully over the years in granting Just the time to carry out his research at Woods Hole and elsewhere.

In 1930, Ernest Just decided not to return to Woods Hole. He gave up his teaching position at Howard, a post which had meant so much to him, and went to Europe to continue his research. Dr. Just had decided to leave the United States, where the doors of major research facilities were so often closed to him because of racial prejudice and discrimination.

Frank Lillie knew Ernest Just better than most men did. In a tribute to his former student and collaborator, published in *Science* (January 2, 1942) shortly after Just's death, Dr. Lillie spoke of a brilliant scientific career. But it was a career, Lillie said, that had been hampered by the effects of prejudice:

> An element of tragedy ran through all Just's scientific career due to the limitations imposed by being a Negro in America, to which he could make no lasting psychological adjustment in spite of earnest efforts on his part.
>
> The numerous grants for research did not compensate for failure to receive an appointment in one of the large universities or research institutes. He felt this as a social stigma, and hence unjust to a scientist of his recognized standing. In Europe, he was received with universal kindness and made to feel at home in every way; he did not

experience social discrimination on account of his race, and this contributed greatly to his happiness there. Hence, in part at least, his prolonged self-imposed exile on many occasions. That a man of his ability, scientific devotion, and of such strong personal loyalties as he gave and received, should have been warped in the land of his birth must remain a matter for regret.

Just certainly appreciated Lillie's contribution to his development as a scientist. This was perhaps shown best by the fact that, during one summer, he cut short a study in Naples, Italy, in order to return to Woods Hole. Many of the people whom he had known and worked with during his years at the Biological Laboratory were surprised to see him. He had shown up unannounced to participate in a special seminar in honor of Dr. Lillie's sixtieth birthday and fortieth anniversary at Woods Hole.

Dr. Just spent most of his last 11 years at famous European research laboratories: in Germany, at the Kaiser Wilhelm Institute for Biology in Berlin; in France, at the Sorbonne and marine stations; and in Italy, at the Naples Zoological Station.

But all of his appointments to these laboratories were limited in time. He never had the security of a life appointment adequate to carry out his work.

In November 1938, in Paris, France, Dr. Just finished writing his second book, *The Biology of the Cell Surface*. In this book, he brought together his life's work on the fundamentals of living cells.

The publication of Just's second book marked a fitting climax to his brilliant career as a research scientist. For only two years later, in 1940, Dr. Ernest Just passed away in Washington, D.C.

"Keyed to the Outside World"

In his new book, Dr. Just summarized his numerous investigations. His investigations focused on only one type of single living cell—the egg—and its development into a complex multicelled animal.

From these investigations, Just developed a general answer, or theory, about a very simple question: What is life? The answer to this question is really the ultimate goal of all biologists.

Dr. Just placed emphasis on the cell material lying around the outside edge of the cell and just inside the cell membrane. This region of the cell is called the ectoplasm. Most biologists up to Just's time had neglected the role of the ectoplasm and had centered on the nucleus of the cell as the "kernel of life."

Just's attention to and definition of the ectoplasm was unique. He saw the ectoplasm as standing between the inner substance of the cell and the outside world. It reacts first to a stimulus outside the cell and serves to condition the behavior of the whole cell.

Thus, ectoplasm, by its location in the cell, becomes important in the expression of life processes, according to Dr. Just.

For example, some of Just's experiments had shown the role of ectoplasm in the intake and output of water from animal cells. Other experiments showed that 1) in an egg without ectoplasm fertilization could not take place and 2) that in cell division after fertilization the ectoplasm affects the formation of a new cell membrane.

Ernest Just's observations and deductions led him to emphasize the role of ectoplasm. He was not saying that this region of the cell was the basis of life. Neither did he think that life rested in the nucleus or genes alone. Instead, he believed that life existed only when all cell parts and their activities were combined and worked together as a unit.

Just's point was that the role of ectoplasm is a prime factor in cell development and growth. In other words, he regarded the surface of the cell as something more than a porous membrane.

The ectoplasm, Just wrote, "is keyed to the outside world as no other part of the cell." Dr. Just observed that it is the ectoplasm that "stands guard over the peculiar form of the living substance, is buffer against the attacks of the surroundings, and the means of communication with it."

There have not yet been any African Americans who have revolutionized man's thinking through science like an Einstein, a Darwin, or a Newton. To date, a Nobel Prize has not been awarded to a person of African descent for work in science.

Dr. Just strove hard, not for prizes or acclaim, but only to prove himself as a man in search of "the truth" through science and for the benefit of all people.

In doing so, Dr. Ernest Just perhaps has come the closest of any African-American scientist to revolutionizing our thinking about the nature of living substances.

MATTHEW A. HENSON

4

The date of July 20, 1969, is historic in space science. On that day, two American astronauts first landed and walked on the moon. Millions of Americans sat in front of their television sets, awed and thrilled as they watched Neil Armstrong and Edwin Aldrin walk on the moon's surface. This first voyage to the moon was one of the most exciting and significant moments in science. But if you had been a youngster in 1909, just 60 years before the first man walked on the moon, you would have been equally awed by man's exploration of the Earth.

In the early 1900s, some men were exploring the ice and snow of the Earth's surface around the North Pole. At that time, the feats of Arctic explorers were as dramatic and daring as those of today's astronauts. Expeditions to the unknown and ice-capped land above Canada were as dangerous then as voyages to the moon or to the bottom of the sea are today.

An outstanding achievement in the exploration of the Earth's surface occurred on April 6, 1909. On that date, two American explorers reached the Earth's geographic North Pole. The temperature was 29 degrees below zero.

The first person ever to reach the North Pole was an African American. His name was Matthew Henson. About 45 minutes later, Admiral Robert E. Peary, a Navy engineer and the planner and commander of the polar expedition, joined Henson at the pole.

At the pole, the latitude is 90° north, so every direction they stepped in was south. North, east, and west had vanished for Henson, Peary, and the four Eskimos who accompanied them to the pole.

Get a globe of the Earth and find the North Pole. Take a quick look at the Arctic land of ice and snow and the seas around it. Can you find Greenland? Imagine yourself surrounded by hundreds of miles of nothing but snow and floating glaciers. Use the scale on the globe to figure out how many miles your home is from the North Pole.

Matthew Henson had been Peary's assistant on each of his explorations since 1888, the first being to Central America. Peary and Henson had exposed themselves to the fierce stress of the Arctic climate on six different trips to the region's icelands.

Reaching the pole satisfied a dream that Peary and Henson had held for 18 years. The North Pole was one of the last major points on the planet—and the most distant one—for humankind to reach. For four centuries before Henson and Peary made their successful expedition to the North Pole, other explorers had tried—and failed. Some lost their lives in the attempt.

An explorer is a special kind of scientist. He or she has the urge to know the unknown, the desire to discover some undiscovered region of the universe. This urge is so strong that explorers risk their lives to find out what lies on the other side of the ocean, to see the strange creatures that live at the bottom of the sea, or to go beyond the Earth's atmosphere.

This urge pushed Marco Polo across Asia, Jacques Cousteau beneath the oceans, Neil Armstrong and Edwin Aldrin to the moon—and it pushed Matthew Henson and Robert Peary to the North Pole.

In their role as scientists, explorers have to take their laboratories along with them. A ship can be a laboratory; so can a spacecraft, or an outpost on the desert or at the North Pole.

Today, the polar ice caps continue to be the scene of scientific interest. Researchers live and work in laboratory stations in both the Arctic and Antarctic regions. Some scientists are studying polar weather. Others are studying long cylinder-shaped samples of ice obtained by drilling into glaciers to depths of 7,000 feet or more.

Just as there are similarities between the missions of astronauts and the treks of North Pole explorers, there are also differences. Henson and Peary did not take much food along, for instance. They hunted and fished for their food while on their expeditions. Walrus were killed to feed the dogs that pulled their sleighs. The astronauts, on the other hand, take their food precooked and in neat packages. (Their problem is keeping weightless meals from floating around inside the spacecraft.)

Another interesting comparison is how slowly the news of the discoveries spread in 1909 in comparison to 1969. The world did not learn of the North Pole discovery until five months after the event. Yet when astronauts stepped down on the moon, hundreds of millions of people the world over watched the actual event on television. It takes only 1.3 seconds for radio waves to travel from the moon to the Earth.

More than 60 years separate Henson's achievement from that of the first moon astronauts, but they shared the same dream of discovery, the same quickening of the heartbeat that comes to explorers when they reach their goal. Before 1909, the North Pole was as remote as the surface of the moon seemed before Apollo 11. Henson and Peary filled in one of the last empty spaces on the globe. (The South Pole was finally reached in 1912.)

A Childhood of Adventure

By training, Matthew Henson was not a scientist. Like many African-American boys and girls born in America in the 1800s, he was able to get only a little education. He never went to high school. He had no college degree.

When Peary first asked Henson to accompany him on an expedition to Greenland, Henson replied, "I'd like to go, but what is there for me to do? I'm not a scientist." Little did he know what lay ahead.

Matthew Henson had spent some adventurous years as a boy preparing for that famous day, April 6, 1909. He was born on a farm in Maryland at the end of the Civil War. His mother died when he was two, his father when he was eight. At 11, to escape an unhappy life with his stepfamily, he ran away to Washington, D.C., to find an uncle he had never met.

Young Matthew found his uncle and lived with him for several years. The uncle sent him to school. When his uncle could no longer care for him, Matthew left to work as a dishwasher in a small restaurant. Working at the restaurant, he heard customers talk about the docks at Baltimore and the large ships that sailed all over the world from there. This talk gave him an urge to see the world and to seek adventure as a sailor.

At 13, Matthew quit his dishwashing job and hiked to Baltimore, where he signed on as a cabin boy on a ship bound for Hong Kong. The voyage took several months. The captain of the sailing vessel began to teach young

Henson how to read and write. Each day, the captain's cabin became a classroom for his cabin boy. The captain also taught Matthew seamanship, navigation, geography, and mathematics. Young Henson learned how to apply first aid to sailors injured aboard the ship.

Henson lived on the oceans for five years. These were important years in his life, though he did not realize it at the time. He became an able-bodied seaman, sailing to China, Japan, Manila, North Africa, Spain, France, and through the Black Sea to southern Russia.

His travels introduced him to many languages and cultures. He learned how peoples of different lands lived and how to live with them. One winter, his ship was locked in a Russian harbor by ice. During this winter stopover, Henson learned to speak Russian, hunt wolves, and drive sleighs through the snow.

When the captain—his first and only real teacher— died at sea, Henson left the ship that had been his home for five years. At 17, he went to Newfoundland on a fishing boat and then on to Boston, Providence, Buffalo, and New York City, working at various odd jobs. At 19, he returned to Washington, D.C., and took a job as a stock boy in a men's clothing store. That job changed Henson's whole life and the history of world exploration.

A Tropical Adventure

In 1888, Robert E. Peary was a civil engineer for the U.S. Navy. He had made a trip to Nicaragua in Central America to lay out the route for a shipping canal between the Atlantic and Pacific oceans. In 1886, searching for adventure, he had traveled toward the Arctic on a whaling ship, getting off in Greenland. He spent several months surveying Greenland's icy coast.

This first Greenland experience made Peary anxious for another trip north. He wanted to be the first man to cross Greenland on foot. Back in Washington, he could find no support for this venture from either government scientists or the public.

The following year, Peary was assigned again to the Nicaraguan canal project. His ideas about returning to Greenland had to be put aside for a while. In preparation for his return to Nicaragua, he went to a store that sold clothes suitable for the warm tropical climates of Central America. He needed a tropical sun helmet.

Matthew Henson was in the back room of the store taking a stock inventory when Peary entered. The store owner called back to Henson to bring out a sun helmet. The store owner knew Peary well and had told him earlier about the excellent work of his stock boy.

When Henson came out with the helmet, Peary introduced himself. He began talking to his new acquaintance. Peary informed Henson about the canal survey job to be finished in Nicaragua and asked him if he wanted to go along with him. Henson quickly accepted this opportunity to travel again.

The survey team spent seven months in Nicaragua. During this time, Henson showed that he had many skills and much ingenuity. Peary made him a field assistant to the surveying crew. This was the beginning of a 23-year-long association in which Henson and Peary worked and traveled together. Matthew Henson would go to the frozen lands of the Arctic six times with Peary, in the years 1891, 1893, 1897, 1898, 1905, and 1908.

While in Nicaragua, Henson learned of Peary's desire to cross Greenland and one day to reach the North Pole. Upon returning from Central America, Peary asked Henson to go to Greenland with him to explore the icebound wilderness of the far North.

Robert Peary had no financial backing for his second expedition. Henson agreed, however, to go without pay whenever Peary was ready. To Henson, the mission was more than an opportunity for adventure. It was also an opportunity for Matthew Henson to explore the unknown regions of courage and determination within himself.

Learning from the Eskimos

In June 1891, Henson started on his first trip to the Arctic region with Peary. The purpose of this expedition was to cross the northern region of Greenland from the west coast to the east coast.

Seven people—including Peary, Henson, a doctor, a bird watcher, a geologist, a skier (who was looking for adventure), and Peary's wife—left on a ship from New York. They carried with them food (tea biscuits, pea soup, dried beef, and fruit), cooking equipment, tents and sleeping bags, and scientific equipment (thermometers, compasses, photographic supplies, a barometer, and a pocket sextant).

In late July, Peary's party stepped off their ship and onto the rocky shore of McCormick Bay in Greenland. The ship was to return for them a year later.

The fall and winter were spent making preparations for the march across Greenland in the spring. Henson set to work building a wooden house that would serve as headquarters. He built the sleighs that would be pulled by dogs over the ice and snow. The dogs were obtained from the Eskimos, who traded them for hunting guns and ammunition.

When the winter storms let up, Peary and the skier set out to cross the Greenland ice cap. Everyone wanted to go, but Peary decided that a small team could travel faster than a larger one and less food would have to be carried. So Henson and the others remained behind.

Henson spent most of his time with the Eskimos. He became a close companion to the Eskimos he met. He learned to speak their language, dress in their clothes, live in their homes, and eat their food.

Hunting, trapping, and fishing on the frozen lands and water were some of the things that Matthew Henson learned to do well. Henson knew that if he were to survive in this land of bitter cold, he would have to learn from the natives. The knowledge and skills that Henson acquired were used to help all of the people in his party. Peary himself depended heavily on Henson's skills, knowledge, and work.

As summer passed and Peary and his traveling companion did not return to headquarters, the waiting party became worried. Henson pictured Peary having fallen into a crevasse in a glacier and his body lying buried in the snow. During the first week in August, the ship returned to carry the party home.

Still, there was no sign of Peary. Henson readied a rescue team. But before he could set out in search, Peary and his companion returned. They had been triumphant, making a round trip of about 1,200 miles. The pair was exhausted, weakened from exposure to the frigid climate, and near starvation.

Back in the United States, Peary began making plans for another trip to the Arctic. He and Henson went on a lecture tour around the country, telling people about their Greenland expedition. Reaching the North Pole was now foremost in their minds.

The North Pole itself was just a pinpoint; it was the region around the pole that was important. Humankind and science would not be satisfied until someone walked within a few miles of the pole. No one knew how it was to be reached. Could explorers get there by way of Greenland? What lay beyond the drifting floes of polar ice?

A Second Try and "Stones from Heaven"

In June 1893, Henson, Peary, Peary's wife, and eight others traveled north again. A large crowd cheered the explorers as the ship pulled away from a dock in New York City. Newspapers carried enthusiastic stories about this expedition. Peary planned to go farther north than he had on his last trip.

Arriving in Greenland on August 3, the party began preparations for the coming winter and spring. A house was built near the shore of Bowdoin Bay. Henson built sleighs to carry supplies. During the fall, trips were made far inland to leave supplies along the ice-cap trail that was to be traveled during the spring march. The supplies were marked by wooden poles driven into the hard snow.

Weather conditions were very severe. The party leaving supplies was turned back by raging snowstorms. A huge piece of glacier fell into the bay and smashed small boats holding barrels of fuel oil for the winter months. Many barrels were lost in the icy waters of the bay. When winter set in, the advance supplies had not been set up on the inland ice. Without these food and fuel supplies, chances of reaching the pole in the spring were not good.

Nevertheless, in March 1894, Peary set out for the interior of Greenland. At one point, 125 miles from home base, the temperature dipped to 40 degrees below zero. Fierce winds and blinding snow made traveling practically impossible. The winds and temperature were more than the sleigh dogs could stand. Many froze to death. Several members of the party were crippled by frostbite, and Peary was forced to return to headquarters. It took six weeks for his weakened and exhausted men to recuperate.

This first year had brought many hardships and disappointments. All but three members of the original party decided to return to the United States in August 1894. Henson, Peary, and a young man by the name of Hugh Lee remained to spend another winter. During the winter season of 1894 and 1895, they discovered three meteorites that they had heard the Eskimos talk about as "stones from heaven."

Peary and Henson had learned something important from their first year of defeat—the field party, to reach the pole, would have to be small. During April 1895, Peary, Henson, and Lee crossed the 450 miles of the ice cap of northern Greenland with three sleighs and 37 dogs. They wanted to map the far northeastern region of Greenland. Peary wanted to know whether Greenland extended to the North Pole or whether there was a frozen sea between Greenland and the pole.

The rugged condition of the country made exploration difficult. Food supplies ran low. On June 25, the three men arrived back at home base with only one sleigh and one dog. Some of the dogs had been killed and used as food by the men. Lee, sick and crippled by the cold, was pulled into home base on a sleigh pulled by Peary, Henson, and the one remaining dog. This expedition had been a long struggle to stay alive.

The explorers gained an important bit of knowledge from this trip, too—Greenland was certainly an island. A sea of ice floes lay between it and the pole. They knew the next expedition would have to be longer, maybe three or four years.

In August, their ship returned to bring them home. With them, they carried two of the three meteorites discovered during the past winter. The third was too heavy to manage aboard the ship. Their scientific prizes also included walrus hides and other animal specimens that had been captured by Matthew Henson. Henson busied himself skinning the walrus during the voyage back to New York.

The meteorites were placed on display at the Museum of Natural History in New York City, where they can still be seen today. Henson went to work in the taxidermy department of the Museum of Natural History. He was now a recognized expert on the Arctic—its weather, landscape, and animal life.

At the museum, Matthew Henson was responsible for mounting the walrus skins and arranging true-to-nature exhibits of the animals and backgrounds of the far North. He helped to plan exhibits of Eskimo villages, showing their skin tents and the snow igloos they used while out on hunting trips.

Henson worked at the museum for two years. In the summer of 1897, he returned to Greenland with Peary to bring home the third meteorite. It weighed 70 tons and was the largest meteorite known at the time. Today, it too can be found at the Museum of Natural History in New York City.

On their voyage back with the huge meteorite, Peary and Henson talked about their determination to reach the North Pole. After returning with the meteorite, Henson went back to his museum work, and Peary traveled to London, England. There, he received a medal from the Royal Geographical Society and a ship for his next journey to the pole.

Henson was still working at the museum when Peary called him in the spring of 1898. Henson had done well at the museum, and he enjoyed his work. He was thinking of marrying and settling down for the first time in his life.

Peary asked Henson once again to leave with him in July for a polar attempt. He was planning to take along only Henson and a doctor. This was his preference despite objections from some of his supporters about his taking a black man with him. Some people thought that Henson should be replaced by a white man.

Try, Try Again

In the summer of 1898, Peary and Henson headed north again. They were hoping to make it to the pole this time. The next four disastrous years were spent in regions above northern Greenland.

Peary had planned to push his ship into the Arctic Ocean. He wanted to use the ship as a base from which to travel to the pole. But short of the Arctic Ocean, the ship became locked in ice for the winter.

This was the expedition's first serious setback. The group had to carry supplies over land to set up a head-quarters at Fort Conger, 400 miles from the North Pole. Fortunately, housing had been built and was intact at Conger, having been left by a previous group of Arctic explorers. The ice of the Arctic Ocean lay between Fort Conger and the pole.

While crossing the ice cap to Fort Conger in January 1899, Peary's feet froze. His toes were severely frostbitten.

The pain in his feet put Peary in agony. Gangrene set in, and the doctor had to remove seven of his toes. Henson cared for Peary during the painful ordeal of waiting for the stumps of his toes to heal. All attempts to reach the pole that season were abandoned.

By March 1900, Peary had recovered, and he and Henson made another drive northward. Only one Eskimo would dare go with them. Peary's crippled feet made the march slow and troublesome over the sea ice. Again, they were forced to turn back.

In the spring of 1901, they tried again. Supplies and food gave out. Their sleighs collapsed. For the third time, they had to turn back to home base.

In 1902, Peary, Henson, and seven Eskimos made another try. They ran into storm after storm of blinding snow. On April 21, they were still 343 miles from the pole. The Eskimos feared the storm and turned back. The dogs broke down under the strain. Food supplies reached low levels again. Peary and Henson were forced to turn around a fourth time and head south. They returned, dejected, to New York in August 1902.

Although Peary and Henson were discouraged, they had been able to make maps of regions that were largely unknown. They had finally learned that the route to the pole by the northwest coast of Greenland was impossible, and they had discovered some new techniques of traveling over sea ice.

During the next three years, Robert Peary made plans to reach the pole again. He had a ship built with engines powerful enough to smash through the ice-clogged seas. Henson took a job on a railroad and traveled throughout the United States.

Northbound Again

In July 1905, Peary's new ship was ready, and Peary, Henson, a doctor, and a weather expert were northbound. By September, their ship reached a latitude of 82° 27' north. This was the farthest north any vessel had ever penetrated the icy Arctic waters.

At the edge of the Arctic Ocean, the team settled down to prepare for the intended spring expedition to the pole, which was about 500 miles away. In early spring, they began the long march across the iced-over ocean with 22 Eskimos, 20 sleighs, and 131 dogs. Matthew Henson took the lead to leave supplies and find the best trails for others to follow.

The ice packs began to melt and break apart early. This made the going treacherous. Many times, they stood at the edge of an ice pack facing open water. The march couldn't continue until the water froze over.

Furious storms forced delays and caused a loss of traveling days. The group succeeded, however, in reaching a point of 87° 6' north latitude, breaking a record for polar expeditions. They were 125 miles from their goal. No one had ever gone so far north. Hardships, hunger, and cold forced them to turn back.

The return journey was a hard one, too. Two blades broke off the ship's propeller. The rudder was damaged from smashing into an ice pack. Water had poured into the ship through a hole made when the stern hit a point of ice.

On Christmas Eve in 1906, the expedition entered New York harbor aboard its battered ship.

This was to have been Robert Peary's last attempt to reach the pole. However, within days of arriving home, he had announced his intention to return for another try. In March 1907, the Peary Arctic Club decided to support Peary for one more try. Peary immediately arranged to have his ship repaired.

The repairs were to have readied the ship to sail that summer, but work schedules fell behind. The postponement gave Matthew Henson time to get married. Soon after his honeymoon, Henson returned to take charge of the ship's repairs.

One Last Try

On July 6, 1908, the ship was ready to steam out of New York for the North Pole again. Henson had waited a year and a half for this day. He had been married about a year, and leaving his wife was difficult. He hoped that the next time she saw him, it would be with feelings of joy and happiness—that she would be glad she had permitted him to leave her despite knowing that he might not return.

Peary took five men with him in addition to Henson. There were the ship's captain, Robert Bartlett; a surgeon, Dr. J. W. Goodsell; a secretary, Ross Marvin; and two young explorers, George Borup and Donald MacMillan.

The ship had been re-named in honor of President Theodore Roosevelt. On July 7, the *Roosevelt* stopped at Oyster Bay in Long Island Sound. There, the president came aboard to add his words of encouragement to Peary and his party. They were off!

The ship headed straight for Greenland. By August 12, the team had reached Etah Harbor on the west coast of Greenland. The trip, so far, had been uneventful. The expedition went ashore to trade with the Eskimos, offering clothing in exchange for whale and walrus meat, dogs, and animal skins.

Henson was so busy on board that he couldn't keep his diary up-to-date. Peary was constantly saying, "Matt, do this," and "Matt, do that." The Eskimos were a problem because so many wanted to come aboard and stay. Forty-nine Eskimo men, women, and children were allowed to remain. They were good workers, even the children.

It took 21 days of fighting almost impassable ice to go north from Etah to Cape Sheridan. Henson worked on the sleighs to be used that winter. The Eskimo women made the clothing for the men to wear during the winter. Small lifeboats were packed with food and supplies in case the *Roosevelt* was lost.

At Cape Sheridan, Henson continued working on the sleighs, which were to be different from those used on the earlier expeditions. Fresh meat was a necessity, and hunting musk oxen and reindeer took many hours. Also, the dark winter days were quickly approaching, and preparations had to be well advanced while there was still light.

All winter long, small parties were moving provisions and equipment to Cape Columbia, the next advance base, 93 miles to the northwest. The trail from the ship (at Cape Sheridan) to Cape Columbia was kept open all winter by the constant travel between the two points. Loads of supplies were left at Cape Columbia.

There were frequent storms and intense cold. Henson saw rocks weighing at least a hundred pounds picked up and blown to distances of more than a hundred feet by the wind during snowstorms.

On February 18, 1909, Matthew Henson and a small group of Eskimos left the *Roosevelt* at Sheridan for the long march to the pole. The ship's captain and doctor had gone ahead to Cape Columbia. Falling snow, which was loose and deep on the ground, heavy winds, and intense cold made the going slow. The travelers slept in igloos at night. Even the Eskimos suffered from the cold, and some turned back. The frozen big toe of one Eskimo was thawed by placing it under Henson's bearskin shirt and against the heat of his body.

Bubbles in the thermometers that the expedition had brought made them unusable, but when the brandy began to freeze, the men realized that it was at least 45 degrees below zero. On February 22, the expedition at last reached the advance base at Cape Columbia.

Peary and the remainder of his party had not left the *Roosevelt* at Sheridan until February 21. While waiting at Cape Columbia for his arrival, the team readjusted the sleighs' loads. Gale winds had destroyed the igloo built earlier, so a new one had to be constructed. The scene was bleak when Peary arrived on February 26.

The Farthest Point North

From Cape Columbia, Henson and Peary were to leave the land and cross 430 miles north, over an ice-covered ocean, to find the pole. Peary wasted no time. Preparations were made carefully, and assignments were given to each member of the party and the 24 Eskimos.

There were six teams. Captain Bartlett and Borup left separately with their teams on February 26 to lay down the northward trail and build igloos along the way. Bartlett was the first off. Borup returned after three days to start out again with a new load of supplies. At 6:30 A.M. on March 1, Henson and his team took the lead, following the trail laid by Bartlett. Marvin, MacMillan, and Peary broke camp later on.

After traveling a quarter of a mile on foot at the outset, each team left the land ice and moved onto sea ice. The sea ice was much rougher. Pickaxes were needed to forge their steps ahead. Sleighs broke easily on the rough trail and had to be repaired in sub-zero temperatures. Strong gale winds blew continuously. The extreme cold numbed their cheeks and noses.

While one team slept, another was able to catch up with it. Then, the first team moved on while the team behind them slept. These marches went on for 14 days.

On March 14, Peary sent his first support party back to Cape Columbia on land. Dr. Goodsell, MacMillan, and four Eskimos made up this first returning party. Temperatures had been 50 degrees below zero, and MacMillan had a frozen heel. Peary's general plan was to continue like this. At the end of a certain number of days, parties would turn back to the land and the ship. By the end of March, all the team members had returned except Bartlett, Peary, Henson, and seven Eskimos.

On April 1, Bartlett and his Eskimo team went the farthest north that anyone had ever been. They went to 87° 47' north latitude to blaze the trail for those who would make the forward march to the pole. While waiting for Bartlett and his team to return, Peary, Henson, and four Eskimos picked out the strongest dogs and rearranged the supplies on the sleighs. They were able to get some 30 hours of rest.

Bartlett finally returned and described with pride his march to the farthest point north. He told Peary what to expect up to that point. Bartlett and his Eskimo aides then bid Peary and Henson good-bye.

As Bartlett journeyed back to land, Henson and Peary headed for the pole. They planned five quick daily marches of 25 miles a day. Peary was in fairly good condition. Up to this point, he had brought up the rear and had used the trails made by his support parties.

On to the Pole

The sun was constantly on the explorers' backs in a never-ending day. A southeast wind was pushing them on. Each day, Peary and Henson became more tired. Their bodies ached. The shifting ice was dangerous. When they finally reached Bartlett's farthest point north, they were still 133 miles from the pole.

On April 4, they were 60 miles from the pole. Henson moved ahead now as the trailblazer. Peary and the four Eskimos followed. On April 5, Peary made an observation with his instruments—they were only about 35 miles from the pole.

No sextant was accurate enough to show the exact pinpoint that was the North Pole. Just how close a person had to be to the pole to claim that he had reached it was a matter of opinion. Most scientists felt that if a person came within 10 to 20 miles of the pole, this would be close enough to claim the pole. The North Pole is a pinpoint in the middle of a huge mass of shifting ice. The exact point may be atop an iceberg one day, a spot on the surface of a pool of water on another day, and a point on a ridge of snow on another.

The night of April 5, 1909, was sleepless for Henson and Peary. Only the Eskimos slept well. Henson and Peary were too excited to sleep. On April 6, Henson was the first to break camp. Peary followed more slowly with three of the Eskimos. The long daily marches and the lack of rest had drained his body of energy. At one point, he was an hour behind Henson. He was able to keep up only by covering most of the distance riding in one of the sleighs.

At about 10:00 A.M., Henson stopped his march. He felt that he had covered enough miles to have reached the pole. Henson and his one Eskimo aide began to build an igloo. Peary with three Eskimos caught up to Henson 45 minutes later. He unpacked his observational equipment and took careful measurements of the sun's altitude. His calculations placed him at 89° 57' north latitude. Ninety degrees north would be the true top of the world. They knew that it was impossible to locate 90° north exactly with the instruments they had.

This was it. They were within the region considered by scientists to be the North Pole.

Later in the day, after sleeping three hours, Henson and Peary moved several miles beyond this first measured latitude. Peary took another observation and found that they were south of the North Pole. They turned around and returned to the igloo for a night's rest. The only direction they could move in was south.

The next morning, April 7, the explorers made more observations of the sun. Photographs were taken of the icy terrain. Weather observations were written down. With a sounding instrument, they recorded the depth of the polar sea to be greater than 9,000 feet at the point where they were. As Peary called out the measurements, Henson recorded the figures.

Later that day, Peary photographed Henson and the Eskimos holding flags. Henson held the American flag.

The Most Qualified Person

Matthew Henson risked his life, as did Peary, to claim the pole for the United States. Upon their return home, Henson lectured about their discovery while Peary wrote a scientific report to prove that they had reached the pole. His report was sent to the National Geographic Society. After his lecture tour, Henson wrote about his adventure in a book titled *A Negro Explorer at the North Pole.*

Why did Peary select an African American to go with him to the pole rather than one of his white assistants? This might seem like a foolish question to ask, but it was a question asked many times after Peary, Henson, and the other members of the support party had returned to the United States. Some people criticized Peary for taking Henson rather than Captain Bartlett.

Undoubtedly, most of the critics lacked a real understanding of the problems of polar work and travel. Most were ignorant of the entire history of polar exploration and what Henson and Peary had gone through and learned together in more than 20 years.

Few people knew what it meant to travel over the rough ice of the polar sea. There was no understanding of how sleighs had to be built for the rough conditions of travel in Greenland or how food and fuel had to be carried. There was no understanding of how to drive the dogs or how to feed them and keep them healthy. There was no understanding of how to dress in order to withstand the bitter Arctic temperatures.

This knowledge could only be acquired through actual work. There was no opportunity to practice in laboratories, as today's astronauts do before their long missions into outer space. Lack of understanding of the skills required of a man to reach the pole was perhaps the main reason why people criticized Peary for taking Henson with him. They did not realize that Henson was the only man who had mastered all of these skills.

Matthew Henson first went north with Peary in 1891. He accompanied Peary in 1893 over the Greenland ice cap. Together, they rounded the northern end of Greenland in 1900. Henson shared with Peary four heartbreaking years from 1898 to 1902. He helped Peary break the record for going the farthest north in 1906. Henson always got along well with the Eskimos, and the Eskimos' assistance was essential to Peary's mission. Henson built the sleighs and repaired them. Several times, he saved Peary's life.

During the winter of 1909, while still on board the *Roosevelt*, Peary told MacMillan about his plans for the polar attempt to be made in the spring. He told MacMillan that after each man had traveled to a certain point, he would return to home base. But, said Peary to MacMillan, "Henson is not to return. I can't get along without him."

And so Matthew Henson became co-discoverer of the North Pole. He had been indispensable in this great and daring discovery, and he had made a unique contribution to science.

Matthew Henson belongs to that small and special group of searchers who have given us greater knowledge of our world.

GEORGE WASHINGTON CARVER

5

In January 1921, an African American stood before the Ways and Means Committee of the U.S. House of Representatives in Washington, D.C. From a cardboard suitcase, he pulled out bags, tubes, and bottles containing many products made from peanuts, including the ones listed below:

Butter	Wood filler	Oil
Soap	Meat sauce	Linoleum
Breakfast cereal	Leather dyes	Shaving cream
Face cream	Bleach	Paper
Dried coffee	Plastics	Ink
Wood stain	Synthetic rubber	Candy

Some 30 small bottles held dyes made from peanut skins. Another bottle held a creamy peanut butter. Still another held face cream made with a peanut oil base. The bags contained food for cattle, instant dried coffee, and breakfast cereal. There was ice cream powder that could be mixed with water and frozen, like ice cream made from dairy cream. And there was milk, too, made from peanuts. This special milk had been given to starving babies in Africa, where animal milk was scarce.

The man who was proudly presenting these products was George Washington Carver, an agricultural scientist. "Gentlemen," he addressed the committee, "I have been studying the peanut. All of these products before you were made with substances taken from the peanut. They were developed in my research laboratory at Tuskegee Institute in Tuskegee, Alabama."

George Carver had come to the nation's capital at the request of the United Peanut Growers Association. The congressmen were considering a tariff bill that was to give protection to American crop farmers. The peanut growers wanted peanuts included in the tariff bill. Rice, peanuts, and other food crops grown in China and Japan were selling for less money than products grown in the United States. This competition seemed unfair to many American farmers. A tax on imported food crops would make the prices of foreign foods equal to the prices of crops grown in the United States.

For three days, the members of the committee had listened to people talk about rice, or wheat, or tobacco protection. Carver was the last to be heard. Listening to a black man from the South talk about the possibilities of the peanut was the last thing the congressmen expected. After all, the peanut plant was considered a worthless weed. Peanuts were something to eat at the circus or a baseball game. Some congressmen thought Carver and his peanuts were just a joke to end the long days of hearings.

Carver was to have talked for only 10 minutes. But he captured the attention of the congressmen and was allowed to speak longer and to answer many questions. He spoke of sweet potatoes and exhibited some of the products created from this crop—ink, pomade (an oil for hair), mucilage (a sticky glue), relishes, and flour. He held up a bottle of syrup made from sweet potatoes: it could be used to hold peanuts together in a peanut candy bar.

But the scientist from Tuskegee went back to talking about his peanuts. He claimed they had more possibilities than sweet potatoes. He explained how the lowly peanut was one of the richest products of the soil. It was rich in nutrients and had chemical substances that could be used in various industries.

The peanut, Carver said, could keep hungry people healthy and make southern farmers wealthy.

"I have even made artificial meat dishes from peanuts. As science develops the products of nature, we are going to use less and less meat," George Washington Carver continued. (Today, some meat companies in the United States are producing artificial meat products using plant fibers from soybeans.)

At the end of this last day of testimony, George Carver walked down the steps of the U.S. Capitol building alone with his heavy suitcase in hand. He headed back to his small and simple laboratory at Tuskegee Institute. In a later meeting, the congressional committee did, in fact, vote to include the peanut in the new tariff bill.

Peanuts were no longer just "peanuts."

The "Plant Doctor"

George Washington Carver was an extraordinary man. His life had been extraordinary, too—difficult and sometimes cruel.

As a young boy, he had been raised by a white farmer and his wife, the Carvers, in Diamond Grove, Missouri. George's mother, an enslaved woman who worked for the Carvers, was kidnapped from the Carver farm by slave raiders before George was a year old. His father, a slave on a farm near the Carver's, was accidentally killed before his mother was taken away. George and his older brother never knew their own parents. Farmer Carver gave them his name.

George grew up lonely and sickly, but with a very curious and intelligent mind. He wanted to know everything there was to know about plants and animals.

However, George Carver had no science books, and there were no nearby schools for black children. So the young boy had plenty of time to roam the woods and fields around the Carver farm. He learned much by studying nature in the wild. Plants became his toys, and animals were his playmates. He picked flowers, grasses, and fruits; he collected frogs, grasshoppers, and tree bark. George would ask himself questions: Why is grass green? What are flowers for? How does a seed make a plant? Why do plants die?

When George found plants that were wilting or dying, he would dig them up, bring them home, and nurse them back to health. He did this alone and quietly in his secret garden. During the cold winter months, George Carver protected his plants from the cold by caring for them inside a barn. Neighborhood friends of the Carvers called him the "Plant Doctor."

George was in love with nature. He believed that God would tell him everything he wanted to know about plants if he carefully and patiently cared for them. Young George was a keen observer, able to see more in plants and flowers than others could. This ability was later seen in his very detailed paintings and drawings of plants.

At 10 years of age, George Carver struck out on his own to get an education. He wandered in poverty about the countryside of Missouri and Kansas, attending school and working as a farm hand, cook, and laundry helper. In Minneapolis, Kansas, George settled down to attend and graduate from high school.

At every chance, George worked among plants and flowers. Unable to have his own permanent garden, he began to draw and paint. The lifelike details of his paintings showed how carefully he observed nature and how much he knew about plants.

At 25 years of age, George Carver gained admission to Simpson College in Iowa. (In his first attempt to attend a college, he was rejected because of his race.) George continued his painting at Simpson, and his desire to study botany grew stronger.

Despite Carver's ability as a painter, his art teacher felt that a black man could never make a living as an artist. When she learned of Carver's interest in botany from his paintings and achievement in science courses, she wrote to her father, a professor of horticulture, at Iowa State College.

After two years at Simpson College, George Carver was admitted to study in the agricultural department at Iowa State College. Carver worked in the greenhouse and laboratory to earn his living money and tuition. When he wasn't working, he was studying botany, chemistry, mathematics, bacteriology, zoology, and entomology.

Carver continued his painting, too. His love for plants and skill in painting helped him to win several prizes for his drawings at the Iowa Exhibit of State Artists. One of his paintings was sent to the World's Fair at Chicago, where it won an honorable mention award.

In 1894, George Carver graduated from Iowa State College with high honors. He remained at Iowa to study for his master's degree in botany and agriculture.

Because of Carver's outstanding work with plants and soils, he was made an assistant instructor in botany and was appointed director of the greenhouse. His passion for plants deepened. In cross-fertilization, the propagation of plants, mycology (the study of fungi), and plant diseases, Carver did outstanding work.

In 1896, when George Washington Carver received his master's degree, his research in agricultural science was becoming widely known. Other scientists began to look to George Washington Carver as an authority.

In 1897, Carver reported a new kind of taphrina, a fungus plant that grows on the leaves of red and silver maple trees. Years later, this species of fungus was given the scientific name *Taphrina carveri* after its discoverer.

Make Something of It

In 1881, Booker T. Washington, an African-American educator, became the first president of Tuskegee Institute, a new school for blacks in Tuskegee, Alabama. In 1896, Washington asked George Carver to become head of the school's new Department of Agriculture.

This job involved directing agricultural research and teaching natural science to southern farmers, who needed help urgently at that time. These poor farmers would be taught how to use the soil more effectively and how to grow and harvest a variety of crops in order to support their families.

George Washington Carver agreed to join the faculty at Tuskegee Institute. It was there that Carver eventually became famous and, in turn, helped make Tuskegee (now known as Tuskegee University) as famous as it is today.

When George Carver arrived at the school, there was no laboratory space or scientific equipment to work with, as there had been in Iowa. While Booker T. Washington had wanted such an agricultural laboratory, there was little equipment or money to establish one.

Washington's new teacher-scientist, being quiet and shy, liked to work alone, and so he asked for a room of his own for a laboratory. Today, in the George Washington Carver Museum, you can see the crude laboratory equipment that Carver made for his first laboratory.

Carver's philosophy was to start with what you have and make something of it. For heat, he adapted an old barn lantern. A heavy kitchen cup became his mortar, a vessel in which to grind up substances. A flat piece of iron was used to pulverize substances placed in his mortar. Carver made beakers by cutting off the tops of old bottles found at the dump. An ink bottle was soon turned into an alcohol lamp. And from plant fibers Carver made a wick for his lamp. Out of George Carver's small laboratory at Tuskegee came discoveries and products that enriched the southern farmer, the whole of America, and eventually, the world.

During Carver's first year at Tuskegee, Washington persuaded the Alabama state legislature to finance the Tuskegee Agricultural Experiment Station. George Carver was made director of the station. He began to demonstrate how science could be used to benefit the farmers by showing them new ways of fertilizing soil and planting seeds.

The things that George Carver learned at the station were used to help southern farmers—black and white—to prosper. Carver helped the farmers in several important ways—by detecting and fighting plant diseases, by finding new techniques for soil conservation and fertilization, by making medicines from plants, and by raising healthier livestock. Farmers traveled for many miles to learn from George Washington Carver.

One of George Carver's greatest accomplishments was in persuading farmers to grow crops other than cotton. Cotton had been raised in the South for more than a hundred years. Easy to grow but difficult to harvest, the cotton crop was the basis of the South's economy. Cotton was shipped to factories to be spun into cloth. Before the Civil War, slaves were used to build the cotton industry. They planted, picked, and cleaned the cotton by hand.

After the Civil War, which ended legal slavery, cotton continued to be the main farm industry. Ex-slaves who became tenant farmers and the white plantation owners for whom they worked continued to depend on cotton for a living. Most blacks still lived and worked on plantations and farms. This was unfortunate since food was scarce, especially for poor black people. The many years of growing cotton—and nothing but cotton—had ruined the soil.

The cotton plants use up large amounts of minerals, draining the soil of nutrients. So after years and years of planting cotton, a good cotton crop was hard to grow. This one-crop system bothered Carver. He knew that farmers needed to find other crops to grow instead of cotton, such as green vegetables. Vegetables would not leave the soil a wasteland after harvesting. But it was not easy to convince farmers that other crops would serve them better.

Carver wanted the farmers to plant a crop that would grow well in poor soil and, at the same time, add nutriment to the soil. The peanut plant was his choice.

The surface of the roots of this plant have swellings called nodules. Bacteria that live in these nodules take nitrogen particles from the air and convert them into useful plant material. When these roots are plowed into the soil after harvesting, they enrich the soil with nitrogen substances. Carver's science, however, could not persuade the farmers to try peanuts. The few who tried growing them switched back to cotton.

It took the boll weevil to convince Alabama's farmers that growing crops other than cotton was a good idea. This beetle fed on the cotton plant and laid its eggs in the beds of cotton. The eggs of this pest developed into larvae that fed on the fibers of young cotton. The weevil larvae began destroying acres upon acres of cotton, just as they had done earlier in Texas, Louisiana, and Mississippi.

The ruin brought on by the boll weevil forced the southern farmers to stop raising cotton. They were finally ready to try peanuts, as George Washington Carver had long been recommending. (North American farmers had been familiar with the peanut for some time. Slave traders used peanuts to feed people who were brought to work on the cotton plantations.)

The peanut harvest was a large one, but the market for peanuts was small. More peanuts were grown than could be sold. Besides, peanuts from the Far East were being imported and sold in America for less money than

American-grown peanuts. Acres of peanuts rotted in the ground—and Carver received much criticism. He faced a real dilemma. What could be done with all the surplus peanuts that he had talked the farmers into growing in place of cotton?

Making a Market for Peanuts

Being the scientist that he was, Carver decided that he would take the peanut apart. He wanted to know what it was made of. What would it be good for? He sought to find new commercial uses for the peanut.

In his lab, George Carver began to shell peanuts by the handful. Saving the reddish peanut skins and broken shells, Carver ground the peanuts themselves into a fine powder. He heated the powder and then put this peanut mash under a hand press. An oily substance dripped into a cup beneath the press.

Carver then heated this oil at various temperatures to see what happened to it. The oil was also broken down into other substances, which Carver used to make soap, cooking oil, and rubbing oil for the skin.

By adding certain chemicals to the dried peanut cake that remained in the press, Carver extracted a substance similar to cow's milk, though it had less calcium than animal milk. From this milk, he was able to make cheese.

Next, Carver removed the dried, crumbly peanut cake left in the press and placed it into a glass vessel. He added water and enzymes. The enzymes were substances that would help break down any proteins in the peanut. This mixture was placed in a warm-water bath to activate the enzymes. By this technique, the different proteins in the peanut were separated, and Carver showed that a pound of peanuts contained the same amount of protein as a pound of beefsteak.

When George Carver wasn't teaching his classes, he spent long hours separating the various substances that make up the peanut. He was taking the peanut apart chemically. This left the scientist with simpler substances, such as water, fats, oils, gums, resins, sugars, starches, pectoses, lysin, and amino acids. Carver then recombined these materials, under different temperatures and pressures, with other substances. This process resulted in new foods, medicines, and other basic products. From the red peanut skins, Carver made a thin paper. From the shells, he made a soil conditioner and insulating board.

As the years went by, Carver worked ceaselessly in the same laboratory room that Washington had given him in 1896. He kept adding to the list of products that he had made from peanuts. By 1943, the year of his death, his investigations had led to the creation of more than 300 products from the peanut. Carver also developed more than 100 products from the sweet potato, such as paste for postage stamps and envelopes. And from the clay in Alabama soils, he produced colorful dyes and paints that could be used in the home and in industry.

For more than 46 years at Tuskegee, George Carver worked virtually alone and unaided. Unlike most scientists of today, he had no team of scientists or laboratory technicians to help him with his investigations. It wasn't until 1935 that Austin Curtis, his only assistant, joined him at Tuskegee. Carver had very little monetary support. His laboratory equipment was never fancy or expensive. Much of it he made himself from discarded junk.

George Carver showed that plant life is more than just food for animals. As you know, plants use sunlight as a source of energy to make such substances as sugars, fats, and proteins. Carver analyzed plants to find out what they were made of. He then combined these simpler, isolated substances with other substances to create new products. He prepared more than 500 dyes from 28 kinds of plants.

The branch of chemistry that finds ways to use raw materials from farm products to make industrial products is called chemurgy. George Carver was one of the first chemurgists and one of the greatest of all time.

Today, the science of chemurgy is better known as the science of synthetics. Each day of our lives, we depend on and use synthetic materials made from raw materials. All his life, Carver battled against the disposal of waste materials and warned of the need to find substitutes for the natural resources being used up by humankind.

Carver's Legacy

Carver did not care about getting credit for the new products he created. He never tried to patent most of his discoveries or get wealthy from them. (He did, however, receive three patents for chemical processes to produce cosmetics, paints, and stains.) He turned down several offers to leave Tuskegee Institute to become a rich scientist in private industry.

Thomas Edison, inventor of the electric light, offered George Carver a large sum of money to work with him. Henry Ford, the inventor of automobile fame, offered him a laboratory to carry out research on food substances. And when the U.S. government made him a collaborator in the Mycology and Plant Disease Survey of the Department of Agriculture, Carver accepted the position with the understanding that he wouldn't have to leave Tuskegee. (An authority on plant diseases, especially of fungus plants, Carver sent hundreds of specimens to the U.S. Department of Agriculture.)

At the peak of his career, Carver's fame and influence were known in every continent. People near and far wrote thousands of letters asking his opinion on scientific questions and seeking the privilege of working with him in his laboratory. Frequently, the professor from Tuskegee would not accept any money in return for the suggestions that he gave or the various scientific problems that he solved for businesses and individuals around the world.

The peanut industry is indebted to George Carver for demonstrating the commercial usefulness of peanuts on the world market. The U.S. Department of Agriculture, through its Southern Utilization Research and Development Division in New Orleans, Louisiana, continues to conduct research on peanuts, sweet potatoes, soybeans, and other vegetables. The substances that give peanuts their flavor and aroma are being studied, too. Through methods far more complicated than those Carver used, new protein substances have been discovered in peanuts and peanut flour. The food industries are interested in using these substances for the development of new foods for the consumer market.

The United Nations Children's Fund is interested in peanut products as a source of protein to feed hungry people in places where the supply of protein-rich food is less than adequate. Research has established that peanut flour is a food quite high in protein. Only a few ounces of a peanut-based protein powder per day in the diet will raise the body's protein content to an adequate level to maintain health.

George Washington Carver, through the creation of synthetic products from plants, contributed to the rebirth of agriculture in the South and the entire country. Today, his contribution continues, thanks to the Carver Research Foundation at Tuskegee University in Alabama.

A few years before his death, Carver donated his life savings of $33,000 to establish the George Washington Carver Research Foundation for the continuation of his work in creative research. The purpose of the foundation was to provide facilities and support for young African Americans engaged in scientific research.

After Carver's death, the rest of his estate went to the foundation, making his total contribution $68,000. Gifts of money also poured in from friends, and eventually a research building was erected for the study of agricultural chemistry, plant diseases, mycology, and plant genetics.

Over the years, hundreds of young men and women have studied and carried out advanced research at the foundation. Giving these young, gifted minds a chance to carry on research was one of Carver's most important and meaningful contributions. The Carver Research Foundation has made great progress in promoting the study of scientific agriculture at Tuskegee. Though work in the area of chemurgy as such has not been done since Carver's death, large grants of money from government agencies have allowed the foundation to move into broader and more modern areas of study.

For many years, the research foundation has been using isotopes (radioactive materials) as a tool for studying plant physiology. Cesium-137, an isotope, has been used by the Department of Food Technology to study the effects of ionizing radiation on perishable foods. The foundation has studied the soil factors affecting the absorption of radioactive strontium by plants, the persistence of pesticides in soils, hormones responsible for the flowering and fruiting in plants, and the feasibility of growing different plants in the Alabama soil. Such studies, extending the frontiers of knowledge in agricultural science, stem from the inspiration and humanitarian spirit of George Carver.

"Being Helpful to the World"

George Carver received many medals, citations, and honorary degrees for his achievements in research and for his contributions to the improvement of health and living conditions of southern people. The National Association for the Advancement of Colored People (NAACP) awarded Carver the Spingarn Medal for distinguished service to science. Simpson College, Carver's alma mater, awarded him an honorary degree of Doctor of Science. Carver was even made a fellow of the Royal Society, Britain's most prestigious scientific organization.

On January 5, 1943, George Washington Carver died at Tuskegee Institute. He was buried on the campus near the grave of Booker T. Washington, Tuskegee's famous founder and the man who brought Carver to the institute. George Carver never married and left no known relatives.

In January 1945, the U.S. Congress made Carver's birthplace a national landmark. In 1948, the United States honored him with a postage stamp with his picture on it.

Today, near the Tuskegee University chapel stands a curved stone seat. Carved into a marble slab lying within its arc is this inscription:

George Washington Carver

A life that stood out as a gospel of self-sacrificing service. He could have added fortune to fame but caring for neither he found happiness and honor in being helpful to the world. The center of his world was the South where he was born into slavery some 79 years ago and where he did his work as a creative scientist.

PERCY L. JULIAN

Percy Julian was one of America's premier chemists. As director of research for a major chemical company and, later, as founder and president of his own company, Julian Laboratories, Julian was a pioneer in the synthesis of chemicals used in both medicine and industry.

Percy Julian's scientific work ranges from developing a new substance to snuff out gasoline and oil fires to synthesizing the drug cortisone (a drug that eases the pain of people with rheumatoid arthritis). During his lifetime,

Julian was awarded more than a hundred U.S. patents for his chemical products and processes. Two of Julian's patents are for his synthesis of the male and female sex hormones—testosterone and progesterone.

Percy Julian once remarked, "I have had one goal in my life—that of playing some role in making life a little easier for persons who came after me." But life was not easy for him.

As an African American, Percy Julian faced a world of racial prejudice and discrimination in twentieth-century America. Such prejudice presented him with challenges as difficult as the scientific breakthroughs that he succeeded in making. And his approach to his work as a scientist and to his world beyond the chemistry laboratory was shaped by the hardships and obstacles that Julian faced along the way to becoming a world-renowned scientist.

"Not for You!"

The fact of rigid racial segregation in the deep South affected Julian at a young age. Montgomery, Alabama, was his birthplace. His father, James Julian, son of an ex-slave and a railway mail clerk, demanded perfection from his oldest son, Percy, and his five other children. When young Percy scored 80 on a math test, he arrived home proud and excited.

His father, however, gave him a harsh, but loving, scolding for not scoring 100. "A son of mine must not be satisfied with mediocrity," James Julian said, for he knew that if his son wanted to be a scientist, Percy would have to work doubly hard to excel in a world where skin color was used to keep African Americans from getting a good education. He knew that Percy needed to meet the highest standards to compete in a world where skin color was used to keep African Americans in menial jobs.

But the standards set by Percy Julian's father were not matched by the standards at schools for blacks in Montgomery at the time. Segregated schools controlled by whites were of poor quality. There were no science classes to spark interest and talent in science for Percy Julian and his classmates. With his interest in science, Percy once climbed high up on an iron fence to watch students working in a chemistry lab at the all-white Montgomery High School. A policeman pulled him down off the fence and ordered him home, saying, "This is not for you!"

At the time Percy Julian finished elementary school, there was no public high school for black students in Montgomery. Education for blacks was not encouraged in the South. So Julian attended the same mission school attended by his father. The school had been founded after the Civil War to educate the children of ex-slaves. With the support of his mother (who taught school) and his father, Percy Julian became an outstanding student. But the mission school was not challenging enough for such a bright and ambitious student, and so he transferred to the State Normal School for Negroes, in Montgomery.

In 1916, when Julian was a 17-year-old high-school student, St. Elmo Brady became the first African American to receive a doctoral degree in chemistry. The news of such an achievement by an African American reached aspiring black youth through the black newspapers or *The Crisis*, a magazine published by the National Association for the Advancement of Colored People (NAACP).

Young blacks at the time waited with excitement to read the names of African Americans who had earned their college degrees. These announcements meant a great deal to young people like Percy Julian. Julian later recalled their importance:

> The inspiring news of St. Elmo Brady's degree reached me in the summer of 1916 at my home in Montgomery, Alabama, as I was applying for admission to college without ever having attended an accredited high school. . . .
>
> Brady's accomplishment strengthened my determination to attend college, and—what was a miracle to me—I was admitted in 1916 to DePauw University in Greencastle, Indiana, on probation and as a "sub-freshman." I remained a "sub-freshman" for two years while I carried high-school courses in the remnants of the old Ashbury Academy, along with my full program of freshman and sophomore work. . . . I also waited tables for my meals, fired furnaces for my room rent, and played for dances with a little jazz orchestra to help pay my way.

By the time Julian reached his junior year at DePauw, he had full-fledged college standing. And by the time he graduated in 1920, James Julian's son had the highest grade point average among the 160 graduates. He was valedictorian at the graduation ceremony.

Percy Julian had worked diligently for four years at DePauw, with the inspiration of St. Elmo Brady urging him on. His desire to continue studying in chemistry was as strong as ever. With the highest grades in his class, Julian had been elected to the prestigious Phi Beta Kappa academic fraternity. It was customary for the head of the Department of Chemistry to find graduate fellowships for students who had excelled as Julian had and who wanted to go on for an advanced degree.

Percy Julian waited anxiously to hear from Professor W. M. Blanchard about a fellowship for advanced study and research. White students were passing in and out of Blanchard's office saying, "I'm going to Michigan," or "I'm going to Yale," or "I'm going to Ohio State."

"Where are you going?" they asked Percy Julian. "You must be getting the Harvard plum!"

"I could stand the suspense no longer," Julian later recalled. He confronted Professor Blanchard and asked, "Did you get me a fellowship?"

Professor Blanchard responded, "Now, now, Julian, I knew you would be asking me that. Come into my office."

The professor showed his best student letters from several American chemists who had written to caution the young man against a scientific career. One of the letters read as follows:

> I'd advise you to discourage your bright colored lad. We couldn't get him a job when he's done, and it will only mean frustration. . . . In industry, research demands co-work, and white boys would so sabotage his work that a research leader would go crazy. And, of course, we couldn't find him a job in a white university. Why don't you find him a teaching job in a Negro college in the South? He doesn't need a Ph.D. for that!

Julian's dreams were shattered. He pressed his lips together to hold back the tears. He had wanted to be a chemist since the day that a policeman had pulled him off the fence overlooking the chemistry lab in a school that blacks could not attend. Again, he was being turned away because of his race.

"Don't be discouraged," advised Professor Blanchard. "President Fayette MacKenzie of Fisk University is visiting tomorrow, and I'm sure he will give you a position."

MacKenzie did arrive the next day, and Percy Julian went off to Fisk University—a well-known black college in Nashville, Tennessee—to teach chemistry under Professor Thomas Talley. It was Talley who had sent St. Elmo Brady off to graduate school at the University of Illinois, where he had earned a doctoral degree.

While disappointed that he was not going to work on an advanced degree in chemistry, Julian was determined to make the best of the situation. At Fisk, he was pleased to find ambitious and bright students who challenged him as an instructor. However, being a teacher was not what he wanted to do.

So, in 1922, Julian applied for a fellowship to Harvard University in Cambridge, Massachusetts. His old professor at DePauw supported him despite the fact that Blanchard still thought that Julian would not find any doors open to him in chemistry because of racial prejudice.

Percy Julian was admitted to Harvard on a fellowship. He was awarded his master's degree in organic chemistry in 1923.

The boy from Alabama's poor and segregated schools, now with an advanced degree from prestigious Harvard University, was on "the track" he had dreamed about. Yet, while graduating at the top of his class at Harvard, just as he had at DePauw, Julian was not given the research-teaching position that was usually awarded to the best students. Officials at Harvard felt that whites would not accept him as a teaching assistant.

For several years, Julian labored at minor research tasks. Then, in 1926, he obtained a teaching position in chemistry at West Virginia State College, a college for black students. When he arrived at West Virginia State, Julian found a chemistry laboratory with hardly any equipment. He found no assistants to help him continue the kind of research that he had been doing at Harvard.

But with the interest and full support of the college's president, Julian developed a chemistry lab. He plunged into his research during the evening hours, after teaching classes all day. As the only instructor in chemistry, Julian had to be the laboratory storekeeper and janitor as well, working well beyond midnight, day after day.

Imitating Nature

While at Harvard, Julian had become interested in how carbon atoms are bound and linked together to form the basic "building blocks" of the substances that make up living things. These substances are called proteins. Plants and animals produce these substances, and they are useful in treating diseases and body malfunctions. But plants and animals only produce them in small amounts. Getting large enough quantities of these substances for medical treatment was not practical in the 1930s.

Percy Julian was searching for organic chemicals in natural products. He wanted to understand how living cells are able to turn organic materials into such life-giving substances as vitamins and hormones. Julian's goal was to produce synthetic, or laboratory-made, versions of the substances that were made naturally by the living cells of plants and animals.

Organic substances are rich in carbon. At Harvard, the young chemist learned how carbon atoms group themselves in different formations and shapes to form proteins, the group of substances that are the basic building blocks of the human body. To copy these compounds, to imitate nature itself—this was the scientific challenge that Julian set for himself. This was the scientific mystery that he wanted to solve.

To train himself, Julian began to repeat some of the experiments of Ernst Spath of Vienna, Austria, who had gained fame for synthesizing the drug ephedrine in the laboratory. Ephedrine is used today in decongestants, a medication used for treating the common cold. But the facilities and resources at West Virginia State were not adequate for such research.

In 1927, Percy Julian moved on to Howard University in Washington, D.C., to teach chemistry and pursue his research interests. While building the chemistry program at Howard, he gained the financial support that enabled him to go to the University of Vienna in Austria. There, he was able to study organic chemistry under Ernst Spath. It was Percy Julian's "big break." Working with Spath, Percy Julian finally received his doctoral degree in 1931, nearly 15 years after his role model, St. Elmo Brady, had completed his degree.

While studying in Vienna with Spath, Julian became interested in research on the chemistry of soybeans. He began to explore the emerging field of synthetic chemistry with a special interest in using natural substances from the soybean.

The soybean was being used in European laboratories to manufacture certain drugs. One of these drugs was physostigmine, a muscle relaxer. This drug was useful in treating glaucoma, a condition in which fluid pressure impairs vision and can cause blindness. Using physostigmine to relax the muscles around the eye permitted the fluid to drain away, reducing pressure on the optic nerve at the rear of the eyeball.

Scientists knew the chemical make-up of physostigmine—that is, how the atoms of the drug are arranged—but no one had ever been able to make it in the laboratory. And it was extremely expensive to extract a few grams of physostigmine from soybeans.

Julian returned to the United States and went back to Howard, where he headed the chemistry department. With two assistants from the University of Vienna, Julian began investigations of physostigmine. He published his findings in the *Journal of the American Chemical Society.*

Julian's work soon attracted the attention of other chemists who were working on similar scientific problems. Dean Blanchard invited Julian to return to DePauw to guide the research of senior students and to carry on the work that he had started in Vienna and further developed at Howard University.

Julian accepted the offer from his old professor. It was at DePauw that he accomplished his first breakthrough— the synthesis of physostigmine. After carefully examining the molecular structure of this substance, he sought ways to copy it—in other words, he was trying to produce a laboratory-made substance that was identical to the substance produced naturally by the soybean plant.

Julian's research had to be done between his teaching assignments. In addition, he had to endure the resentment of those people who were upset because DePauw had employed a black person as a faculty member.

But Percy Julian did not give up or give in to those who tried to make his life difficult because of his race. Experiment after experiment was bringing him closer and closer to making physostigmine.

After three years of work, Julian finally developed a synthetic chemical similar to natural physostigmine. Were the two substances identical? The melting points of each chemical would be the test. Identical melting points (the temperature at which solid crystals would turn to a liquid form) would be proof that the substances were the same. If the melting points were different, then Julian would have to continue his quest.

One of Julian's assistants, Josef Pikl, who had come from Vienna to work with him, began to heat the test tube with the natural crystals. Julian heated the tube with the synthetic crystals. Dean Blanchard watched nervously.

"Mine's melting at 139 degrees!" yelled Pikl.

"Mine, too, at 139 degrees!" shouted Julian.

The two thermometers had registered the same melting point. The three men hugged each other for joy.

For scientific breakthroughs to be accepted by other scientists, the researcher must present his or her work for their review. Dr. Julian described his synthesis of physostigmine in the journal of the American Chemical Society. His article (co-authored with Josef Pikl) was titled "The Complete Synthesis of Physostigmine."

At the end of the article, Percy Julian thanked Dean Blanchard. Without his support, Julian said, "this work would have been impossible."

Praise for Julian's work came from eminent chemists throughout the world. Today, physostigmine is a powerful medication used to treat glaucoma and other muscle conditions. Julian solved a scientific puzzle that had baffled some of the world's most brilliant chemists for more than 70 years.

The year was 1932. The Glidden Company in Chicago, Illinois, was interested in current research on the protein-rich soybean. Glidden was a company that manufactured a host of products—paints, varnishes, metals, foodstuffs, and various industrial chemicals. It was the development of paints that attracted Glidden's attention to the soybean.

Casein, a protein, had been extracted from soybeans by chemists working in Japan. This protein was used to coat paper so that ink would hold fast to the surface (and not be absorbed into the paper's surface). Producing large amounts of casein from the soybean was expensive and time consuming, however. As yet, no one had managed to synthesize this important protein.

Knowledge of Julian's work had spread across the country, and he received a telephone call from Glidden's vice president, W. J. O'Brian. Julian traveled to Chicago for an interview and was offered a research position. He accepted and thus began a productive 17-year career with the company, eventually reaching the position of director of research of Glidden's huge soya products division.

Julian's first assignment for Glidden was working out a new process for isolating and preparing various proteins from the soybean. He developed some uses for soybean-derived proteins that had never been available before—a new technique for coating paper and a new chemical for use in a fire-fighting foam.

The fire-fighting foam containing Julian's soya protein put a chemical blanket over gasoline and oil fires, preventing oxygen from fueling the burning process. The fire was doused like magic. The lives of many people were saved by this fire-fighting chemical.

The challenge of making synthetic casein, however, was still facing chemists at Glidden. Julian succeeded in finding a way to develop a protein substance that was similar to casein in its chemical make-up. He went on to design a new factory for producing this synthetic protein. (Glidden's process of preparing protein substances from soybeans was losing $35,000 a year. Julian designed a new chemical process with new equipment. Within a year, the $35,000 loss became a $135,000 profit for Glidden.)

Percy Julian had made another major breakthrough. He received a U.S. patent in 1941 for the preparation of a "vegetable protein." Between 1942 and 1954, Dr. Julian received more than 50 U.S. patents for new chemicals and chemical processes used to develop substances that had important applications in medicine and industry.

Dr. Julian and his staff of chemists at Glidden also worked with soybean oil. This oil is rich in a class of substances called sterols, which are the base substances in the chemical make-up of hormones produced in the human body. Sterols form the male and female sex hormones (testosterone and progesterone). These hormones develop male and female sex characteristics and control the body's production of reproductive cells (the sperm in males and eggs in females).

Sterols are organic compounds that are "hidden" in soybean oil. In other words, it is very difficult to penetrate the oil to remove the sterols. One of Dr. Julian's most important pieces of work was the recovery of sterols from the soybean.

At the time, sterols extracted from the bile of animals were used to treat medical conditions in people whose bodies did not naturally produce enough of the sex hormones. (Bile is produced in the liver and released into the small intestine to aid in the digestion cf fatty foods.) But animal bile yielded very small amounts of sterol. The bile from nearly 15,000 slaughtered oxen would be needed to treat one patient for a year. The solution to having an unlimited supply of these hormones for medical use was to learn how to synthesize them in the laboratory.

Dr. Percy Julian did just that.

Today, synthetic sex hormones have a variety of uses. Progesterone, for example, can help pregnant women who are likely to have miscarriages. Synthetic testosterone is used to help young men whose normal male hormone production may be low at puberty and to treat infertility. Both hormones are also used with some forms of cancer.

Julian's next major achievement was the synthesis of cortisone. Cortisone, a hormone produced by the adrenal gland, is effective in treating the pain suffered by people with arthritis. But like physostigmine, testosterone, and progesterone, the natural supply of this hormone from the soybean was so limited that widespread use of cortisone was not possible. Cortisone was also obtained from animal bile. Here, too, the yield was too small and the cost too high to benefit many patients.

Dr. Julian succeeded in creating a substance that he called cortexolone S. It was identical to cortisone except that it lacked an atom for oxygen in a key position in its crystallized form. But once inside the body, the substance would attach to the oxygen carried in the blood stream. The wonders of cortisone were made available at a cost that made treatment a possibility for many patients.

Today, cortisone is used in different forms to treat different types of inflammation including those of the skin, eyes, bowels, joints, and respiratory tract. People whose bodies produce insufficient amounts of corticosteroids and people who suffer from Addison's disease are also treated with cortisone.

Julian's synthesis of hormones from soybeans ranks among the most important achievements in the history of organic chemistry. His appointment as director of research at the Glidden Company was also a turning point in the acceptance of African-American scientists. Julian headed a staff of 32 chemists.

Many honors were bestowed on Percy Julian. In 1947, the National Association for the Advancement of Colored People (NAACP) gave him the Spingarn Medal, as it had to Ernest E. Just in 1915 and George Washington Carver in 1923. The award was made "to the man or woman of African descent and American citizenship who shall have made the highest achievement during the preceding year or years in any honorable field of human endeavor."

In 1950, Dr. Julian was honored by the city of Chicago for his development of synthetic cortisone. He was named the "Chicagoan of the Year." As the audience rose and applauded Julian, his parents were brought forward from behind the stage curtains. Their appearance was a complete surprise to their now famous son.

In 1951, Northwestern University awarded Dr. Julian an honorary doctor of science degree. The citation that accompanied the degree read, "Education's investment in him has been returned manyfold in the magnificence of his achievements to mankind."

"The Hurt to the Spirit"

Despite his many achievements and the honors that he received over the years, Percy Julian and his family met with racist treatment again and again. Shortly after being honored in Chicago, Julian purchased a new home in the all-white suburban community of Oak Park, near the Glidden Company. The December 4, 1950, issue of *Time* magazine reported the following incident under the heading "The New Neighbor":

> In Oak Park, there were people who attached more importance to the color of a man's skin than to his achievements. . . . Julian paid $34,000 for an ornate 15-room house . . . and began spending $8,000 more for landscaping and improvements, intending to move his wife and children in by Christmas. When the news got out, the water commissioner refused to turn on the water until the Julians threatened to go to court. Anonymous telephone callers made threats.
>
> One afternoon last week, after the landscapers and renovators had gone for the day, a dark sedan pulled up at the Julians' house. Two men got out, broke into the house and poured gasoline through all the rooms. They laid a clumsy fuse of surgical gauze to the outside and lit it; it went out. Then they tossed a flaming kerosene torch through the window and drove away. Before the gasoline was ignited, neighbors called the firemen and the house was saved.
>
> Percy Julian, a proud energetic man of 51, stood his ground and served notice that his family would move into the house by New Year's Day. He hired (for $36 a day) a private, round-the-clock guard to patrol the property with

bulldog and shotgun. "We've lived through these things all our lives," said Percy Julian. "As far as the hurt to the spirit goes, we've become accustomed to that."

A year later, *Time* magazine (July 1951) reported a second incidence of racial discrimination involving Julian. The article was titled "Barred for Reason of Color":

> Naturally, Dr. Percy L. Julian's name was on the list when a group of outstanding industrialists and scientists were invited to a private luncheon at Chicago's exclusive Union League Club last week. After all, Julian is a research director for Glidden Company and the chemist who invented, among other things, a process for the synthetic manufacture of experimental drugs for treating arthritis. But when the Union Club saw his name on the list, it said he could not come to the club. Reason: the club's directors had "issued a rule barring Negroes." . . .
>
> Said scientist Julian, "It appears to me that organizations like the Union Club are as directly responsible as any other agency for such un-American incidents as the bombing of my home. . . . When individuals in high places behave as the Union Club behaves, ordinary citizens [will] follow suit."

By 1954, the chemist who had helped the Glidden Company quadruple its sale of soybean protein and who had led the way in the use of soya sterols to create a host of synthetic substances was ready to strike out on his own. Another chemist had discovered that the Mexican yam (sweet potato) was also a source of sterols for the drug cortisone. With this in mind, Julian started his own research and development company, Julian Laboratories, Inc., in a small concrete block building in nearby Franklin Park, Illinois.

The wild yams of Mexico, Julian soon discovered, were an excellent source of sterols for the cortisone and other products that he began to develop and sell. During his first year of business, Julian's profit was only $70. But the second year was much different—there was a profit of $97,000. Within a few years, Julian Laboratories was a thriving pharmaceutical company, producing a wide array of drugs from the yam.

By the early 1960s, Dr. Julian's business had become so successful that it attracted the attention of a major American pharmaceutical firm, Smith, Kline and French, in Philadelphia. Now ready to move into semi-retirement, Julian sold his company.

The Dreamer

In his last years, Dr. Percy Julian had to fight for his life. At age 75, he was stricken with cancer of the liver. He continued to work from a wheelchair as a consultant for Smith, Kline and French, exploring the possible uses of various organic products.

The chemotherapy for his cancer weakened Julian, but he continued his work. "I am trying to summon the little energy that remains in order to do a little more while I can," he said.

He traveled as much as he could, sharing with others his experiences with modern science and the problems of human society.

For Percy Julian was not just a scientist. He was also a humanitarian.

In an article titled "On Being Scientist, Humanist, and Negro," Dr. Percy Julian wrote about the role of African-American scientists:

> The Negro scientist . . . has bridged the gap between humanism and science, if not always by choice, certainly then by circumstance. Living in a segregated society, or ghetto in the broad sense of the term, he has had to concern himself with the problems of his fellow men as a humanist, while at the same time pursuing his career as best he could as a scientist.

Dr. Julian goes on in the same article to recount how difficult it was for African Americans with training and talent in the sciences to gain teaching positions in universities outside of the southern black schools. He recounts how the public libraries in the South were "out-of-bounds" to black students. He recounts how industry would not hire black people. For these reasons, many blacks before and during Julian's time thought it was foolish to gain a higher education, especially in the sciences. They were more likely to seek a marketable skill.

"But," said Julian, "there were a few dreamers, or fools, who dared to follow their urges toward pure science."

Percy L. Julian was one who dared, one who dreamed. And he was one who succeeded as a major contributor to science in the twentieth century.

SHIRLEY A. JACKSON

7

When Shirley Jackson was 10 years old, her mother read the biography of Benjamin Banneker to her. Banneker, a free African American who lived in the 1700s, excelled in mathematics, studied astronomy, and wrote almanacs. In 1791, Banneker assisted in surveying the land, planning the layout of the streets, and selecting the building sites for our new nation's capital—Washington, the District of Columbia.

"Since I lived in Washington, Banneker's life meant something to me," Shirley Jackson has remarked. She, too, showed an early and lifelong interest in science and mathematical problems.

"I liked math first in elementary school," recalled Dr. Jackson, who, like Banneker, was raised and educated in the Washington, D.C., area.

In 1973, Dr. Shirley Jackson became the first African-American woman ever to receive a doctoral degree from the Massachusetts Institute of Technology (MIT). Her field of study was particle physics. Since 1976, Jackson has been a theoretical physicist at AT&T Bell Laboratories in New Jersey. In 1991, she became a professor of physics at Rutgers University.

Since graduating from MIT, Dr. Jackson has become a leading American scientist. Her research in the area of theoretical physics has been undertaken at prestigious laboratories in both the United States and Europe. Her accomplishments have been recognized by other scientists through her election as a fellow of the American Physical Society and the American Academy of Arts and Sciences.

Physics is the science that is concerned with matter and motion. Matter that is moving or in motion is said to have energy. The mathematical description of matter in motion is the essence of Dr. Jackson's work. Matter or material substances have energy that is stored up and that can be released. Physicists like Dr. Shirley Jackson use mathematics to determine the kind and amount of energy that can be produced from a physical system.

What is the world made of? Scientists like Dr. Jackson have developed ideas, or theories, about the make-up of matter. The atomic theory says that all matter is made up of small particles. These particles are called atoms. An atom is made up of three even smaller basic particles: electrons, protons, and neutrons. These are called sub-atomic particles.

Different forms of matter have different combinations of these subatomic particles. A particle, or atom, of the gas hydrogen would be different in make-up from a particle, or atom, of the metal copper. According to the atomic theory, forces, or attractions, between these subatomic particles hold them together in an atom of a substance. The protons and neutrons are bound closely together in the center, or what is called the nucleus, of the atom, and the electrons move around in space outside the nucleus.

Every substance in the world is made up of a different combination of a few kinds of atoms. Water, for example, consists of a combination of hydrogen and oxygen atoms bound together by forces between them.

While protons, neutrons, and electrons are said to be the basic or fundamental particles of matter, there are other subatomic particles known to scientists, such as photons. Photons are particles that make up light. These particles radiate in a wave-like fashion from certain atoms to produce light.

For Shirley Jackson, studying physics means trying to understand the behavior of the fundamental particles of atoms under different experimental conditions. She is particularly concerned with the behavior of electrons, the negatively charged particles that spin around the nucleus of an atom. The movement of electrons allows certain substances to be conductors of electricity and light. Jackson studies the properties of a group of substances that are known as semiconductors.

Dr. Jackson's job is to observe the way the physical world works. She tries to understand why things happen the way they do. In a piece of copper wire, the electrons of the copper atoms flow easily, making copper a good conductor of electricity (a flow of electrons). Other substances—semiconductor materials, for instance—conduct electricity only under certain conditions. Temperature and light are two of the factors that have an impact on how well these materials conduct electricity.

Dr. Jackson uses mathematics to predict and explain the flow of electrons through semiconductors. "What I try to do," Jackson remarked, "is to add to the knowledge about conductors that other scientists and engineers will need to know as they work to develop new materials to improve our communication technology."

It is a complex and challenging assignment. Dr. Jackson notes that much of her work is done with the help of computers. "I use computers to study materials that could be used themselves in computers of the future," she noted.

Scientists like Dr. Shirley Jackson are shaping the future of our way of life. "But I didn't start out like this," Jackson pointed out. "Actually, I was more interested in the biological sciences."

From Bumblebees to MIT

"When I was growing up in Washington, I used to collect live bumblebees, hornets, and wasps," recounted Dr. Jackson. "No dead insects for me." What did a young girl do with a collection of live bees and hornets?

> I'd keep them in old mayonnaise and Mason jars under the back porch, sometimes having as many as 30 to 40 in captivity at one time. I was interested in their aggressive behavior. Mixing them together in a jar, I would observe how they interacted with each other, bouncing and darting around inside the jars. I would put the bumblebees with the yellow jackets and then the bees with the wasps. I'd feed them different kinds of foodstuff—sugar, honey, salt—to see how their behavior changed.

Did she ever get stung as she collected the insects or moved them from jar to jar?

"Never," said Dr. Jackson. "The first time I received a bee sting was when I was attending a physics institute in Colorado during the summer of 1971. I was walking by some shrubs, and somehow one got me on the finger."

Shirley Jackson's early interest in living things and how they change was supported by her parents. "I was very interested in nutrition. My father, who was a post office employee, helped me with my experiments growing molds and bacteria in our kitchen," she recalled.

Jackson's mother gave the young girl another kind of encouragement. "My mother, a case-worker at a school for emotionally disturbed children, was more literary," said Jackson. "She would read to me stories about famous African Americans—like Benjamin Banneker, the mathematician and astronomer, and Paul Laurence Dunbar, the poet, and Mary McLeod Bethune, the educator.

"School was my thing," recalled Shirley Jackson. "It was the focus of my young life."

It was a life already taken with the world of numbers. "I especially liked and did well in mathematics," Jackson remembered. "I liked to play and make up games with numbers for people to solve. One of my science projects was building a slide rule based on a binary system. Reading, too, was a favorite activity."

But it wasn't just the world of numbers that intrigued Shirley Jackson as she grew up. "I was interested in everything. I'd borrow the maximum number of books allowed from the Petworth Library at Georgia and Kansas avenues near our home," she observed.

When Jackson began attending school in Washington, D.C., the public schools were segregated by law. She can still recall how her bus passed by several all-white schools on her way to the Charles Young School (named for one of the first African-American officers in the U.S. Army).

In 1954, the U.S. Supreme Court outlawed separate public schools for blacks and whites. For a while, Jackson attended an integrated middle school, but her high school had a predominantly black population.

Shirley Jackson was in the honors program. With a number of other girls, she formed a club called "Teens of Personality." It was a study and social group. The girls supported each other's individual academic interests and talents. "We all liked and excelled in different subjects—

English, biology, history," Jackson said. "I was the math whiz and had an interest in science. But I had a lot of interests—reading the classics in Latin, poetry, and history, especially the histories of the great wars of the world. Given my many interests, you wouldn't have necessarily predicted that I'd become a scientist."

When the time came for Jackson to think about going to college, an assistant principal suggested that she take a look at the Massachusetts Institute of Technology (MIT), a prestigious school that stressed mathematics, science, and engineering. That's just what she did—and Jackson liked what she saw.

In September 1964, Jackson's parents drove her from Washington, D.C., to Cambridge, Massachusetts. Jackson later recalled that the only concern her parents had was how a black female student would be treated at a school dominated by white male students and professors.

Shirley was a bit scared, too, but she was excited to be at a place where everyone had the same interests. "I thought that I had arrived in heaven," she said, "but I was still frightened."

Dr. Paul Gray, a former president of MIT, understood Jackson's fears. "In 1964, MIT was not an easy place for a woman, black or white," he noted. "There were probably no more than 30 to 40 women in her entering class."

At first, Jackson was rebuffed by most of the white female students. The seats around her remained empty as she sat eating her meals in the cafeteria. She was not invited to join the study groups that worked on physics problems in the dormitory during the evenings. So Shirley Jackson worked alone in her room.

In class Jackson's ability could not go unrecognized. "I'd do pretty well on the problems," she said. "Others would see my grades and would come to ask me to help them with their homework."

It was when she took the freshman physics course that, according to Jackson, she really got "turned on." She was fascinated with the idea of trying to understand the physical world by using mathematics. This seemed to her to be a perfect marriage between math and science. Jackson decided to major in physics.

Courses at MIT are intense and demanding. Only the most able and hardworking students survive the rigorous study required. Shirley Jackson was a survivor. But there were some tough days along the way. There were lonely times when she was treated differently because of the color of her skin. Jackson was one of very few African-American students at MIT at the time. There were only 15 to 20 black students out of a total student population of more than 4,000. There was only one other black female in her class. The white students would often confuse the two.

Some people at MIT found it rather curious that a black woman would even be interested in physics. Jackson was often asked about her background. One professor informed her that she should not be majoring in physics "because colored girls should learn a trade."

Most professors simply tended to ignore her presence. If Jackson was going to succeed at MIT, she was going to have to assert herself more. "They treated me with benign neglect," she recalled, "until I became more aggressive and made my presence known."

In the spring of her freshman year, Jackson applied for a summer job as an MIT laboratory assistant. It was in the laboratory that Shirley Jackson began to feel more comfortable in the MIT environment.

Assisting in new metallurgy studies, doing electron microscopy, or experimenting with semiconductors—these kinds of firsthand activities expanded the world of physics for Jackson. The laboratory setting became a haven, she commented, when "times got tough."

Still, feelings of depression and isolation came over Shirley Jackson, especially when she was excited about solving a problem or reading something new—and then had no one to share the discovery with. But while there were periods of loneliness and the distraction of racial comments, Jackson felt fortunate to be at such an outstanding school.

She also felt an obligation to help those who were not so fortunate. "I used to do volunteer work at Boston City Hospital," Jackson noted. She worked on a pediatric ward, helping children who had problems ranging from birth deformities to leukemia.

When she would get depressed because of comments or reactions she received at school, Jackson found that volunteering time at the hospital helped, in her words, "to keep things in perspective." Being at the hospital helped Shirley Jackson to cope with the challenge of being a black woman in the world of physics, a world dominated by white men.

But despite the many difficulties that she had to face, all Jackson wanted was to be a scientist. She wanted to contribute to the understanding of the nature of matter in the universe.

Shirley Jackson describes herself as "a fairly focused person." An *Ebony* magazine article in 1974 about her confirms the impression that Jackson was a young woman who knew her own mind:

> There are some people who seem to know exactly what they want to do . . . as if there had never been any question about it from the moment they were born. [These people] are organized, unhurried, unhassled, and unafraid. They accomplish a great deal, have inexhaustible energy, and walk about with the confidence of champions. . . . Dr. Shirley Jackson is that sort of person.

On June 7, 1968, a line of students marched along a path at the center of MIT's campus. The path led to the graduation platform. The students were proud to receive their degrees.

Shirley Jackson was one of the happy students that day. This was to be her first milestone at MIT. Jackson had survived her four years to earn a bachelor's degree and was determined to pursue advanced study in physics, but she was not ready to leave MIT.

Although the years had been stressful ones, and even though Jackson had been accepted for graduate study at other prestigious institutions, there was something else that she felt she needed to do at MIT.

Shirley Jackson wanted to see more African-American students enter MIT, and she wanted to help them to overcome the obstacles that she had faced. Helping others meant as much to Jackson as earning a doctoral degree in physics.

One of Jackson's college activities was organizing and working with MIT's Black Student Union (BSU). As a co-founder of the BSU at MIT, she was concerned that, during her four years at college, the number of African-American students had not increased. Only six or so black students were admitted to MIT each year.

Jackson was committed to changing this enrollment problem, but she knew that it would not be easy. "Blacks and women were essentially nonexistent in the science and engineering fields back then," reflected Dr. Jackson in 1991.

In 1968, the BSU, consisting of about 30 students, sent a letter to MIT's president, Dr. Howard Johnson. The union requested action to increase black student enrollment. A Task Force on Educational Opportunity was set up and chaired by Dr. Paul Gray, MIT's chancellor and, later, the school's president.

This marked the beginning of MIT's active recruitment of minority students. Committees crisscrossed the country to identify able minority students who dreamed of being scientists and engineers. A more open admissions policy, a financial aid program, and academic and orientation programs for incoming non-white freshman students were developed. Former MIT president Gray recently recalled

Jackson's contribution to a more diverse student population at MIT:

> Shirley Jackson was the most significant and important constructive force in our group. She had a special understanding of the difficulty of changing an institution like MIT toward diversity. . . . She brought a special balance to a difficult process of change. . . .
>
> Shirley Jackson stands out in my mind as being one of the best bridge builders during that difficult time. Her manner was always calm, unassuming, and reassuring. All of us—administrators, faculty, and students—are in Shirley's debt for her help in opening MIT up to equal opportunity for black and other non-white students.

Jackson's commitment to a more culturally diverse community at MIT resulted in increased minority enrollment. Shirley Jackson continued her studies at MIT, and she continued her efforts to build bridges across racial lines. Project Interphase, a summer program for incoming minority students established during Jackson's graduate years, still exists today at MIT.

Understanding Matter

In June of 1973, Shirley Jackson became the first African-American woman to receive a doctoral degree from MIT. Her field of study was theoretical particle physics.

In this field of study, according to Dr. Jackson, "one tries to understand the interaction of the basic particles of matter. I worked in what was known as interacting physics, where one uses mathematics to study the forces holding protons and neutrons together in the nucleus of an atom."

During the years 1973 and 1974, Jackson continued her investigations as a post-doctoral student at the Fermi National Accelerator Laboratory in Batavia, Illinois. Named for Enrico Fermi, one of the pioneers in physics, the Fermi Laboratory had been set up by the U.S. Atomic Energy Commission. There, a machine called an accelerator was used to move subatomic particles at high speeds.

At the Fermi Laboratory, Dr. Jackson continued to work on gaining a better understanding of the interactions between the basic particles of matter. While exploring the mysteries of subatomic particles was a challenging problem for Jackson, her biggest problem was gaining respect for her scientific research in a male-dominated profession.

After a year at the Fermi Laboratory, Dr. Jackson traveled to Europe as a visiting scientist at the European Center for Nuclear Research (CERN). At laboratories in Switzerland and Italy, she developed theories to explain the interaction of the basic particles of matter. While working at the Fermi Laboratory, Dr. Jackson had developed a model that described particle reactions. At CERN, she had her first opportunity to use the new model to make some experimental predictions.

Doing research and living in Europe was a rewarding experience for Jackson. "It was easier than living in the United States. There were a lot of tensions here racially," observed Dr. Jackson, "and I was away from this in Switzerland, free to concentrate on my science. I was the only black at CERN, but everybody was international. It was very stimulating, both intellectually and personally."

Dr. Jackson traveled to several European countries—England, Germany, France, and Belgium—lecturing and presenting papers on her research. "Science is more than just sitting at your desk, grinding away at problems," she said. "It's thinking and talking with other scientists."

And Jackson found another opportunity in Europe. It was a chance for some skiing in the Alps of Switzerland, a sport that Jackson had enjoyed while a graduate student at MIT.

After a year overseas, Jackson returned for another year's work at the Fermi Laboratory. Then, in 1976, she received an appointment as a member of the technical staff of the Theoretical Physics Research Department at AT&T Bell Laboratories in Murray Hill, New Jersey.

At Bell Laboratories, Jackson switched from research in particle physics to solid, or condensed matter, physics as her primary research area. Condensed matter physics involves studying many atoms bunched together to form a solid rather than studying single free atoms and their basic elementary particles.

In the Physics Research Department, Jackson studied the electronic and optical properties of substances known as semiconductors. Depending upon its specific make-up of atoms, a metal may be a good conductor (like copper), a nonconductor, or a semiconductor. In a semiconductor, the electrons of atoms are closely bound to the nucleus of the atom. But if energy is forced into the semiconductor, the electrons escape from the pull of the nucleus they are spinning around. Semiconductors are superior to normal conductors because there is a better control over the flow of electrons.

To understand the importance of Jackson's work at Bell Laboratories, an overview of the American Telephone & Telegraph (AT&T) enterprise and its research division— Bell Laboratories—is useful here.

The laboratories of AT&T are one of the world's pre-eminent industrial research facilities. Scientific research conducted there has made AT&T a pioneer in information technology and telecommunications. During its first 60 years, Bell Laboratories provided AT&T with the information needed to design and develop a modern telephone service system.

AT&T research laboratories have made contributions ranging from the development of new lasers to the first communications satellite. Other significant contributions include the solar cell, the touch-tone telephone, a portable FAX machine, and the development of fiber-optic cable for transatlantic communication. Today, the research at Bell Laboratories focuses on three information technologies— microelectronics, photonics, and computer software—that are used to engineer a wide range of complex communication networks.

Just as the field of electronics takes its name from electrons, so photonics gets its name from the photon, the fundamental particle of light. Light energy has advantages over electrical energy. Since a photon has no mass or weight, it can move much more rapidly than an electron. Photons are thus superior to electrons for sending messages through certain materials. Photon research has led to the fiber-optic technology now used in many advanced communication systems.

In the late 1980s, more than half of AT&T's 60,000 miles of communications network was upgraded to fiber-optic technology. The communications hardware—that is, the devices and machines for sending messages—must be programmed by computer software. Software enables the thousands of computers in a communications network to work together.

Basic research is essential for AT&T to develop new advances in telecommunications. Physicist Shirley Jackson is one of the scientists who does such research. She spends a great deal of time investigating the electronic and optical properties of certain materials that can carry much more electrical current than is possible with existing technology. These new materials conduct electricity without resistance and, therefore, generate, store, transmit, and use electricity in a more efficient manner.

Scientists can improve the ability of semiconductors to transmit in a variety of ways: by exposing the material to electric fields, by lowering its temperature, or by applying pressure or shining light on the material. Dr. Jackson adds to the body of knowledge that other scientists and engineers at AT&T Bell Labs need to improve conductors and thus to develop better communication devices.

In studying a physical system like a semiconductor, Dr. Jackson asks a series of questions about the system. She poses her questions as mathematical word-problems.

Then, Jackson performs a series of calculations to predict what will happen under certain experimental conditions. "I model the semiconductor system mathematically," Dr. Jackson observed. "That is, I use math to explain to other scientists what's going on in the things they've observed in the laboratory experiments. If I build a math model, I can predict what will happen when the temperature of the conductor is lowered or what wavelength of light will be transmitted at different temperatures."

Dr. Shirley Jackson is one of very few physicists who works in the field of theoretical physics. Of the 40,000 men and women with doctorates in physics, no more than 20 percent work as theorists. At Bell Laboratories, where some 150 physicists are employed, only 20 or so work in the theoretical area.

Balance in Life

After 16 years of research at Bell Laboratories, Dr. Shirley Jackson became a professor of physics at Rutgers University in 1991. While she still holds her position as a Distinguished Member of the Technical Staff of the Optical Research Physics Department, Jackson believes that now she has the "best of two worlds."

"After being at a place like Bell Labs, you end up with more research ideas than you'll ever have time to work on in a lifetime," says Dr. Jackson. At Rutgers, she can help "more young people advance in science."

Shirley Jackson has received numerous awards over the years. She received the Karl Taylor Compton Award at

MIT in 1970 for outstanding contributions as an under-graduate. The National Technical Association presented her with the "Scientist of the Year Award" in 1973. CIBA-GEIGY, a major pharmaceutical firm, selected her for their "Exceptional Black Scientists" poster series—more than 100,000 of these posters have been distributed to schools, colleges, and libraries to publicize the contributions made to science by African Americans.

Dr. Jackson is listed in *American Men and Women of Science, Who's Who Among Black Americans, Who's Who in the East, Outstanding Young Women of America,* and *Who's Who in Science and Technology.* Her membership in professional associations includes the American Academy of Arts and Sciences, the American Association for the Advancement of Science, the National Science Foundation, and the National Society of Black Physicists.

Shirley Jackson's appointments as a trustee of MIT and a member of the New Jersey Commission on Science and Technology demonstrate the influence that she has gained in the world of science. Elected to her first term as an MIT trustee in 1975, Jackson has been re-elected to the board of trustees several times over the years.

In 1985, Governor Thomas Kean appointed Dr. Jackson to the New Jersey Commission on Science and Technology. (She was re-appointed to a five-year term in 1989.) As a commissioner, Jackson helps to bring together the resources of the state's industries and universities.

While these awards, appointments, and memberships are cherished by Dr. Jackson, the reward she receives from her work with young people is most special to her. Along with her scientific work and family responsibilities (she met her husband, Morris Washington, a physicist, at Bell Labs, and they have a son, Alan), Jackson has kept the commitment she first made at MIT in the 1960s—to encourage more African-American young people to prepare for and pursue careers in mathematics and science. (At present, less than 3 percent of American scientists and engineers are black while the African-American population of the United States is about 14 percent.)

The reward that Dr. Jackson gets for participating in programs to motivate young people is as meaningful to her as the awards she has received for her scientific work. "One wants to be recognized in one's own field by other scientists," Jackson says, "but I also want to have an impact on young people." For Shirley Jackson, being available to young people "gives balance to life."

What does Dr. Shirley Jackson see in the future for communication technologies? What breakthroughs might we expect by the year 2000?

"You can't predict the future," says Jackson. "That's what science is all about. It's an activity of discovery. It's like peeling away the layers of an onion. If I knew what was inside, there would be nothing for me to do. A scientist carries out a series of investigations, and you don't always know what is at the next layer."

"Sometimes, there's a surprise," adds Dr. Jackson. "Science is an interesting enterprise!"

INDEX

ABOUT THE AUTHOR

An educator, historian, and author, Robert C. Hayden is known nationally for his writing, lecturing, and teaching on the history of African Americans. He is the author of *Black in America: Episodes in U.S. History* (1969) and *African Americans in Boston: More than 350 Years* (1991). He was a contributor to *Dictionary of American Negro Biography* (1982). From 1974 to 1983, his weekly column, "Boston's Black History," appeared in the *Bay State Banner* in Boston. In 1986, he wrote a viewer's guide to the television series "Eyes on the Prize: America's Civil Rights Years, 1954 to 1965."

Hayden's first biography for young readers, *Singing for All People: Roland Hayes*, was published in 1989. His other books include *Faith, Culture and Leadership: A History of the Black Church in Boston*; *Boston's NAACP History: 1910 to 1982*; and *The African Meeting House in Boston: A Celebration of History.*

A member of the Executive Committee of the Association for the Study of Afro-American Life and History and president of the Boston branch of the association, Hayden is also a lecturer in the Department of African-American Studies at Northeastern University and in the Black Studies Program at Boston College. In addition, he holds adjunct faculty positions at Bentley College and Curry College.

Hayden is president of RCH Associates, an educational consulting firm that works with school and community groups to develop awareness of African-American life and history and to foster intergroup understanding and communication.

Hayden served as executive director of the Massachusetts Pre-Engineering Program from 1987 to 1991.

From 1980 to 1982, Hayden was employed by the Boston Public Schools, where he held several administrative positions: special assistant to the superintendent, executive assistant to the superintendent, and director of project development. He also served as director of the Secondary Technical Education Project at the Massachusetts Institute of Technology.

From 1970 to 1973, he served as executive director of the Metropolitan Council for Educational Opportunity in Boston and then worked in educational research and development at the Educational Development Center in Newton, Massachusetts.

During the early years of his career, Hayden was a science teacher, a news writer for *Current Science*, and a science editor in the educational division of Xerox Corporation.

Hayden earned his B.A. in 1959 and a master's degree in 1961, both from Boston University. He has also completed two post-graduate fellowships: one in the School of Education at Harvard University (1965-1966), the other in the Department of Urban Studies and Planning at the Massachusetts Institute of Technology (1976-1977).

Robert Hayden is the author of three volumes in "Achievers: African Americans in Science and Technology." This biography series includes *11 African-American Doctors*, *9 African-American Inventors*, and *7 African-American Scientists*. First published in the 1970s, these books have now been revised, expanded, and updated by the author.